Skull Cowboy: Oath of Vengeance

Written By:

Eries Q. Blackburn

Edited by:

Joan Akins

Table of Contents:

Chapter 1: One more time

Chapter 2: Feathers of flight

Chapter 3: Prayer and Blood Jewels

Chapter 4: Sow

Chapter 5: Prayer for your Soul

Chapter 6: Sword and Harkness

Chapter 7: Cult of Christ

Chapter 8: Bone

Chapter 9: Over the Veil

Chapter 10: Goodbye Pastor

Chapter 11: Reaper's Vow

Chapter 1: One more time

    As the moon hide behind opaque clouds darkness covered the sky it was obvious winter was vastly approaching. The early morning air was thick filled with the emerging smell of scorched flesh and burning metal, many homesteads had begun to catch fire. The local Blacksmith's forge housed a raging flame that he ignited in the hopes to smelt down several pieces of nearly rusted metal. Having faith that he could indeed rework the metal the blacksmith fanned his flame until the forge's heat caused him to sweat while the metal he placed inside spit sparks that scotched the loose cotton shirt he wore underneath his cowhide apron. Stepping away from the forge taking off his apron so he could easily pat down his shirt the Blacksmith felt two men grab him by his shoulders dragging him out his smithy leaving the forge unattended. The metal had never stopped crackling and soon more sparks emerged setting fire to everything they landed on. Once the smithy was engulfed in a glowing red blaze nearby homesteads were touched by the growing fire.

    The closest town folk grabbed water pails scooping water from horse troughs frantically attempting to put out the fire this continued until only a slow burning smoke was left. Aiming to make sense of what they were seeing everyone's face started to grow with a mix of concern and worry no one knew where the fire emerged from but they could see the unrestrained damaged it left in its aftermath. Looking at homesteads collapsed in and covered by smoke everyone split into groups sifting through mounts of ash trying to find survivors only to discover the burnt corpses of over a dozen families. Once everyone claimed down they were able to see where the fire originated from and were left in shock seeing it was the smithy.

Storming towards the smithy wanting to have a word with the blacksmith to find out what happen everyone stopped when they came to just a frame struggling to hold its shape. Searching through the ash looking to find a charred body like they did in the homes or worse an skeleton everyone started to believe the fire most of been to hot and destroyed everything even bone. Using what was left of a shovel to dig away ash praying he'd find something one man noticed a trail of blood leading from the smithy this sight proved the blacksmith was no longer present in his work shop. Talking amongst each other some thought the blacksmith fled from the fire he caused getting cut as he left they went on to claim he didn't care enough to even warn them about it and just took off. A select few argued that if the smithy was burning from the inside the smoke would have been too much forcing him to run outside otherwise he wouldn't be able to breathe. The man who found the blood shock his head at the idea of the blacksmith fleeing or even running away from a smoke filled room. He didn't know the blacksmith personally but he had paid for his services many times and these minimal interactions gave him a completely different outlet than the others. When all eyes were on him he gave his thoughts starting off by stating that if the forge was hot enough to catch fire the blacksmith was smart enough to find away to extinguish it before it grew and got out of hand. His second comment debunked the views of those who claimed smoke was at fault, by saying that if smoke did in fact fill up the smithy the blacksmith would of stood his ground and found away to put out the fire and get rid of the smoke. All their opinions were unjustifiable since no one seen when the fire started they just had a strong prejudice against the blacksmith letting that cloud their judgment of him. No one wanted to admit they had been impolite and verbally abusive to the blacksmith each time they requested his services and no one wanted to admit how respectful he had been even after dealing with their ill-mannered and unpleasant actions. His character was kind and he had a generous attitude towards them no matter how they treated him, he always wore a smile and worked the hardest out of everyone in town. Thinking about all those things made everyone loath the conclusions they jumped to because no matter how they tried to turn it the Blacksmith wouldn't have just left a fire burning inside his forge. He always went to the extreme to make sure when he left there wasn't a blazing fire or even warm coals but it was very rare when he left. The only time anyone could remember the blacksmith leaving was when he went to stand outside of Sunday service not being welcomed inside or when he approached the Pastor attempting to offer his services to help fix up the old church house.

Opening his eyes glaring into total darkness John banged his head trying to sit up which prompted him to move his hands around feeling his surroundings. It only took a few minutes for him to notice he was inside a coffin buried deep below the ground but the memory of how he got there was gone. Closing his eyes back trying to think of a way out John heard a soft chime of a bell he noticed the bell sound would ring each time he moved his right hand, rubbing his wrist on the side of the coffin John felt the rope that was tied around his wrist someone wanted to be safe just in case he was buried alive. Knowing their wasn't a soul in town that would come dig him out John went with his only option, bending his knees as much as he could hoping to support some of the weight that came from the dirt thrown on top of the coffin he painfully brought his arms up until they were bent at the elbow. The little space he had kept his punches low powered each time he hit the coffin's roof but he stayed persistent breaking two boards causing dirt to pour down onto him. Thrashing his body so that he would have movement through the dirt that submerged him John managed to get his right arm straight between the coffin boards. Using the dexterity he developed in his hands from being a blacksmith it didn't take long to pull himself out the coffin by bracing on the wooden top breaking it as he pushed. Crawling his way out from the dirt John used a sharp rock to cut the rope from his wrist that was tied to the bell. Getting to his feet feeling disoriented John walked towards town his clothing stained by blood and dirt. As he approached town everyone stood shocked the way he looked showed them the worst had happened to him when the fire broke out they just couldn't believe he was still standing. They all watched as he trenched towards the saloon his mudding boots leaving prints behind him with every step. "Shot of the hardest you got" muffled John his voice softer than a quite whisper he could feel the damage on his vocal cords from the pressure put unto them.

"We don't serve your kind here" remarked The Bartender who was attempting to use an intimidating tone as he looked John over locking eyes with him mouthing the words again *"We don't serve your kind here"* as he spit into a glass cleaning it was a rag that had more stains covering it than it had strains of fabric. The Bartender was a middle age man with black hair cut short, his face embraced wrinkles both from aging and spending a lot of time in the sun. He had visible scaring that covered his hands from having them whipped as a child. His gaze caught John as he approached the bar and he hasn't taken his eyes off him since not even while he cleaned glasses one after the other.

"I'm really not in the mood for this game today" John hung his head in front of The Bartender but never took his eyes off him; he was still slightly unsteady from having just climbed out of a grave and his memory foggy. The only thing he knew was that he wanted a strong drink to clear his head and wasn't going to deal with a Bartender that ultimately thought since he was darker that he was allowed to be refused service.

"I am not in the mood to be serving No Ne…." Just as the bartender begun to say his last word John shoved his hand straight into the Bartender's mouth grabbing his tongue wrenching it down having his face flush with the counter. Fettling around his person using one hand feeling if he had anything on him John pulled a bowie knife out of his pocket and proceeded to impale the Bartender's tongue piercing it to the counter with enough force to crack the wood.

"Anyone else have a problem with me having a drink?" He screamed twisting the knife he gripped in his left hand smiling as the Bartender's screams got louder. Feeling how euphoric the screams were making him John could feel he had a specific purpose but what that purpose was he had yet to find out. Never letting go of the elk antler handle that his bowie knife had John begun to twist the blade again first counter clockwise then back clockwise. Placing the palm of his right hand on the top of the blade's handle John pushed the blade completely through the Bartender's tongue. Just as the screams of pain came flying out the bartender's mouth John had already turned to face the rest of the Saloon. As he looked around the saloon he noticed no one wanted to even look at him they reared their eyes when he gazed at them this didn't bother him one bit he was use to it. The people in the saloon trying to avoid John's gaze were the same people who were determined to prove he had fled from the fire until they really considered how he carried himself even in the face of their belligerent ignorance. They still had the audacity to harbored hatred towards him for how he looked however his recent actions frightened them. He wasn't the peaceful blacksmith that just dealt with their bad-mannered behavior anymore so they didn't won't to meet his gaze out of fear he'd pull a knife on them too. "I didn't think so" said John through smirking lips.

"You're meant to be dead Harkness!" A quite voice echoed from the saloon door way the rasping under tones sent shivers down John's spine as he heard it. Leaping over the counter to get his drink John made sure to knee the bartender in the face as he climbed over. He also thought having some space between him and the man who just entered would be good.

"Do I look dead?" reaching for a bottle from behind the counter John could hear the man as he started to walk towards him. The spurs on his boots clanged in rhythm as he walked.

"Whatever you are thinking boy, you best not" said the man who was mere steps away from the bar he could reach out and touch John if he attempted to.

"I'll do what I please" remarked John as he placed his hand on the counter tapping his ring finger twice and his index finger once. He was mentally trying to contain himself until he got a strong drink

"That's the tone what got you killed in the first place" said the raspy toned man as a placed his hand over his gun keeping his eyes on John's movements

"And here I thought loving the Pastor's daughter is what did me in" grabbing a bottle from the top shelf turning to face the man John watched it shatter in his hand feeling the bullet penetrate his stomach as it exited the bottle. "That's one Waylon"

"Sounds like a threat, you threatening me Harkness?" replied Waylon as he got ready to fire again.

"Damn right but that ain't a threat" reaching to grab a second bottle John lifted it off the shelf upside down anticipating Waylon would shot it which he did "You just love firing that thing don't you"

"Next one goes in your head!" Screamed Waylon aiming his gun right at John's face

"I'm going to get my drink in than I'm going to kick your ass" tilting what was left of the bottle into his mouth Waylon watched as John swallowed not only the liquor that remained but glass shards as well forcing him to take a step back "so about that bullet for my head you going to reload that pistol or you need me to do it for you?" reaching underneath the container pulling out a shot gun "Damn can always count on white folks to have fire arms and they see me as the problem" throwing the shot gun at Waylon's feet before hoping over the container to look him eye to eye "Got the balls or is your courage in your white sheet?"

"I got the courage!" reaching for the shot gun Waylon found his wrist was being stepped on

"You really think I'm going through that again" adding pressure as he turned his heal John listened for the sounds of breaking bone it felt liberating to destroy the hand that fired eighteen rounds into his back. As his altercation with Waylon raged on John started to have memories of his past and what had happened to him. The first memory that replayed in his head was when he was grabbed from his smithy and whipped across the face with the handle of a pistol, the same pistol Waylon had fired twice.

"Harkness you should of stayed dead he will find you" scrambling with his right hand to reach for the shot gun Waylon was kicked to the ground just he a grabbed it "You'll pay for what you did to Estelle and he will bring you to justice". John started to remember how one of the men who grabbed him put bag over his head while another chained him to hitching post. He could only hear their voices as they cracked a whip over his back the more he cried out in pain the more lashing they gave him. Having done nothing wrong John stopped giving them the satisfaction of hearing how much pain he was in and he shut his mouth biting down on his tongue until blood leaked out the edge of his mouth into the bag.

"JUSTICE!" whaled John grabbing his knife from the bartender's tongue "YOU SPEAK OF JUSCTICE WAYLON!" gripping the knife firmly in his left hand he walked towards Waylon who had managed to crawl fair enough away he could take a shot if he tried "WHERE WAS THIS SAME JUSCTICE WHEN AN INNOCENT WOMAN WAS KILLED!" John's nostrils flared his eyes fueled by remorse each step he took echoed he sounded like a thousand horses charging up a hill. "SHE LOVED ME!" he screamed "SHE LOVED ME!" he screamed again as tears filled his eyes "WHERE'S HER JUSTICE WAYLON WHERE IS IT?" lunging with his knife John stumbled back taking four steps before falling into the nearby tables sending glassware and poker chips flying in the air. Everyone stayed silent only the sounds of grunts could be heard as Waylon got off the floor and walked towards to the bar.

"There's your justice Harkness try coming back from that" placing the shot gun onto the counter Waylon picked up his pistol and walked over to where John had fallen seeing that he was laying face down. "They are going to be excited I took care of it on my own this time" using his foot Waylon kicked John's right side hard hoping to ensure he was dead.

"That's two Waylon" mumbled John his voice sounded slurred as though he was biting his tongue as he said each word

"how are you not dead!" Waylon was left stunned his face filled with confusion as he drew his pistol aiming it at John. "That shot should have killed you!" cupping both hands on the handle of his pistol Waylon attempted to steady his shaking, he had never seen a man survive a shot gun blast from that close of range before. In the saloon everyone continued to stay silent as they all glared at John who was using the table he had turned over to brace himself up. Only one

Saloon maiden didn't looked at John her eyes were peering at Waylon she watched his every move mouthing the phrase "Best Run White Boy". Keeping her piercing gaze she moved unfazed by the continuing commotion to the bar where she poured herself two shots of liquor downing them both all while maintaining intense eye contact with Waylon who still stood petrified.

"Life isn't formilar to those who haven't lived" said John finishing his struggle to get up "Death paid me a visit using your invitation so I became formilar with Vengeance" As he turned towards Waylon everyone could see the shot gun had blown a hole clear through his chest "look at this it's my favorite part". As the wound healed in front of his eyes Waylon couldn't hold back how frightened he was any longer causing him to tremble more than he had been. Steadying his breathing Waylon remained a firm grip on his pistol's handle never breaking from his aimed position at John until he watched a wound that should have been fatal heal. That was the breaking point he had lost all control of his composure he could no longer contain his freight which lead to him pulling the trigger of his pistol blowing the right side of John's face clear off sending chunks hurling in different directions like Flesh and bone shrapnel.

"At least you left my good side" remarked John smirking with what was left of his lips as blood poured down his chest covering his clothing and dripping on the floor.

"I was aiming for your whole head" yelled Waylon who was sure that each word exited his mouth with a frightened tone; he knew everyone else could hear it because he himself could. Adverting his eyes from John's bloody mess of a face just for a short second Waylon noticed the saloon Maiden had never left from behind the bar she just kept pouring herself drink after drink, He wondered if she had ever broken her gaze from him. Taking one last glance at her Waylon watched as she begin to shake her head back and forth as she mouthed "Been watching the whole time, You ain't smart, should've ran" reading her lips Waylon swallowed quietly not knowing who he was meant to be afraid of anymore. Returning his gaze back in Johns' direction Waylon believed that the horror scene caused by his pistol wasn't as scary as the saloon maiden. Looking at the floor seeing the large amount of blood he hoped the wound was fatal this time and didn't heal like the shot gun blast John took to the stomach finally lifting his eyes up to John's face Waylon was taken aback by what he saw the wound hadn't healed completely.

"Guess your aim is off" John walked over to Waylon who was now shivering in fear that something bad was about to transpire. Stopping only one step away John gestured face and Neck upwards feeling the last bit of skin heal "Send the Pastor a message for me" quivering worse than he ever had Waylon took the final step towards John

"What's the message?" asked Waylon

"Tell him I will find out who really killed my Love" John's body tensed up he could sense the vengeance building inside him and he loved ever seconds. He didn't know what the feeling was when he attacked the bartender but now he knew it was vengeance and he wanted it more than breathing.

"I can relay that for you no problem" Waylon's eyes darted to a door adjacent to the bar and he begun to consider his options. He thought about finally making a ran for it or if John would really let him live, he even thought about his chances of firing off another shot to buy himself time it wasn't until he could feel the cold of John's body only inches from his did Waylon come to the realization he had no options at his disposal.

"You know on second thought ill…" lifting Waylon and throwing him against the wall John grabbed the pistol he was shot "This tune is about to sound formilar so you best strap in" using his feet to pin Waylon's hands down John aimed the gun aligning it with Waylon's spine unloading the four remaining rounds in the chamber "You fired eighteen shots into my back using impeccable aim having me blood out"

"I was just following my orders I only shot you" felling his body loss blood Waylon knew he wouldn't survive "I wasn't the only one that day so watch your back Harkness" snatching the bullets from Waylon's holster to reload the chamber with six rounds John unloaded them next to the four he already shot into Waylon spine he kept reloading and firing until he got to eighteen. He had taken vengeance on the person who shot him repeatedly by taking him out the same way however as John admired the bullet holes in Waylon's back he couldn't help but wonder why it felt more like revenge than vengeance. Placing his hand around his neck feeling the imprint from the rope that was tied against it infuriated him.

"I'll murder you all! No one will live for what they did! Vengeance will be mine!" snarled John his voice echoing throughout the Saloon

"JUSTIC…." Waylon dropped his head into a puddle of his own blood losing the struggle and dying.

"I will get JUSCTICE for Estelle and I'll search for those who are over do for VENGENCE!" removing Waylon's pistol holster from his dead body John wiped what blood he could off and put it on placing the pistol in the holster as he begin walking towards the door. "Acts of murder are only admired by death himself" Spoke John seeing the bullets he fired had ended up in the shape of a crow on Waylon's bloody back. Pausing at the saloon door John peered at his reflection in a nearby mirror *'This is what I've become all over loving someone dearly'* he thought *'My heart was always hers and for that I was killed Now my heart is no more and I must be the one who kills'* having seen the reflection of his new nature John walked out of the saloon.

Chapter 2: Feathers of flight

Felling the sun beat down on him John found himself with only one option he had to pay the pastor a visit. How he would make his presence known was a different struggle entirely his encounter with Waylon wasn't planned it just happened by chance and John knew he wasn't going to get that lucky when it came to the pastor he was going to have to search for him. Searching wouldn't be hard all he had to do was go down to the church and kick in the door the pastor always stood at the front of the alter no matter the day of week. He claimed that was the only place he truly felt one with God and so he went to the church's alter every time he prayed, the pastor prayed so often that on occasion his wife would jokingly say he loved God more than her. The reply she got was always the same even when she made the joke around guest "I love my God and my wife evenly" the pastor would say with a smile as he brought his hands together and looked up to the sky.

Each time his reply cared less and less emotion towards loving his wife and more towards loving God this caused his wife to grew resentful of their marriage and she begun to loath her husband and the God he believed in. She stopped going to church and never walked down to join him in prayer as she use to. The only thing she did was stay home and tend to their daughter Estelle who had just became a woman and was struggling to find footing with the people In town especially the men who all wanted to turn her into a house wife that would birth them children. As he started walking towards the church John recalled when he first met Estelle she had came to his Smithy looking for service wanting to know what he charged for his labor. Her mother sent her since the importance of the visit was to build new rafters for the church and replace the old decrypted roof that had been worn by the seasons. The first thing he noticed was her flowing black hair that was intertwined into a braid which ran down the spine of her back as she stood in the doorway of his smithy facing away, he could tell she was nervous to come speak with him on her own after all when it came to matters of the church normally the Pastor paid John a visit himself. There had been rare moments when he sent his wife and even then she wasn't alone their eldest son would accompany her and do most of the talking. When the pastor's wife renounced her faith in God she no longer helped with church matters and visiting the local blacksmith was left up to the eldest son who John despised with a burning hatred.

   Even coming back from the dead didn't take that hatred away from John's spirited in fact he felt a compelling urge to go find the Pastor's eldest son and pay him a visit. The visits he paid John when the church was in need of services weren't too friendly and always resulted in the town sheriff throwing John in jail for the night. Every night he spent in jail he fantasized about a new way to murder the Pastor's eldest son and how he could make it look like bandits had killed him, after all the Pastor even with his faith would always pray that God condemn Bandit and outlaws to Hell over what they did to him. That's how every outcome inside John's head ended with the town and church believing bandits killed the pastor's eldest son. Learning from his shoot out with Waylon that he can heal from any wound inflicted on him John turned his sights from the church to the Pastor's eldest son prioritizing petty human revenge over Vengeance for the death of his beloved Estelle.

As he walked down the dusted road he could hear everyone gasping as they looked at him seeing how bloody his clothing was and the fact he was still wearing the nuce he was hung on before being cut down, the frayed end of the rope dangled down his back as he walked paying it no mind. "Thanks for looking….I know" John repeated over and over to everyone that looked in his direction he was becoming irritable with how he was being treated. "You think being murdered would be cause to cut a black man some slack" John remarked to two butchers that were standing out of their shop dressed in leather aprons that were covered with just as much blood as John's clothing. One of the butchers was an elderly man who had grown up working in the shop and later inherited it from his father when he passed, he was the only one in town to have honest respect for John and his contributions, the feisty butcher was the man's son and he shared the same views as the church when it came to John.

"They gave you too much slack boy that rope broke" the young butcher retorted as he stepped down onto the road standing in front of John "You shouldn't opened that mouth" pulling a knife from his waist line the butcher tossed it between hands before being pulled back onto the porch by his father. "What you do that for?" he asked his father making no attempt to hide his disrespectful tone

"That there is the black smith that murdered the pastor's daughter"

"So what that doesn't give him permission to come near our shop you know what they say about his kind and what just having one around does" handing his knife to his father the young butcher walked back into the shop with his head hanging low.

"Glad to see you're a live John" said the elder butcher smiling

"Samuel that boy of yours needs to watch his tone I'm a lot different these days" John stepped onto the porch and grabbed the cigar that was hanging out of Samuel's mouth "I'm dead so I'm taking this" puffing on the cigar John's mind drifted back to his first day with Estelle and how heavenly her voice was radiating with his spirit making him feel butterflies for the first time.

He could see her clear as day as though she wasn't murdered; he could even see the white and black dress she wore upon meeting him and how it floated just above the dirt how she accented it was a red lace ribbon tide around her waist. John felt remorse every time he thought of Estelle now and he felt at fault for not being there to save her when she was murdered. Just as the rope tightened around his neck he was told that Estelle was murdered and the men around him kept asking him how it felt to be a murdered as they laughed watching him claw at the nuce trying to get air.

"John you can be dead but that's mine" Samuel yanked his cigar from John's hands breaking his trace like state "You couldn't handle one of my cigars when you were alive death didn't change that my friend" leaning on a beam to his shop Samuel shock his head at John "You really kill Estelle?"

"I would never kill her!" John snapped his mind being clouded by vengeance once again

"No the good ole Blacksmith would never kill the Pastor daughter, Sure John I believe you" blowing his cigar smoke into John's face Samuel started to laugh loudly "If anyone in this town knew you'd never hurt that girl it was me"

"You had me going for a minute Sammie"

"It was obvious you both were in love everyone could see that" standing up right Samuel stabbed his son's knife into the door frame "didn't feel like holding that" John laughed which to him felt great he hadn't had it easy the last 24 hours and that little action from Samuel was enough to make his day. "Town folk didn't care to much for you loving her, They believed she could always go find one of those strapping white farm boys and settle down" gesturing the cigar to John before pulling it back quickly Samuel pondered over what to say.

"Emphasize on the white part of that White farm boy" John said sarcastically as he rolled his eyes

"You'd be right on that one although it wasn't until she refused to love anyone besides you, that's when they did her in and you got the blame" John stood baffled he was at a loss for words how could Samuel know so much "surprised you're back from the dead though, didn't hear a bell"

"They didn't bury me I was left hanging and bleeding out from being shot" ripping the cigar from Samuel's hand John started smoking it as he sat down "doesn't seem to affect me much" turning to walk inside Samuel open the shop door leaving John sitting on the porch alone. As he sat smoking John contemplated how he was going to murder the Pastor's eldest son since this time wasn't some jail house fantasy to keep him from going insane it was an action that was going to take place. In his mind he could recall every time someone got offended do to the color of his skin and how often they'd threaten to hang him for it. "I should have left this town when I wanted to" said John out loud adjusting the nuce loose enough to take it off and throw it on the ground. "I can't believe I didn't take that off when I first came out the grave, why didn't Waylon just pull me by it?" taking a few more puff before softly blowing off the ash John couldn't think of any reason as to why Waylon didn't attempt to grab him by the nuce. "Guess that white boy was just a Firecracker who only cared to use a gun, Told him he ain't have courage, Boy was I right. Now he's dead and I'm hunting down others for Vengeance without the slightest clue to go on" just as John came to the discovery that had no clue who he was really looking before besides the pastor Samuel walked back out the shop holding a cloth bag in his hand.

"They didn't bury you my friend but you were buried" Samuel tapped John shoulder getting his attention "Come with me" getting up from off the porch John followed Samuel to a small table a few feet off to the right of the butcher shop "you were buried and placed into a grave with a dead ringer just in case"

"I used that dead ringer until I didn't hear the bell anymore" looking at the cloth John grew suspicious as to what it was "I had to claw my way out using my bare hands, Whoever cut me down and buried me must of not cared enough to pay attention to the dead ringer!"

"Don't you dare think caring wasn't involved" Screamed Samuel as he placed the cloth on the table pulling out its contents leaving John with a shocked look on his face "The rest of the nuce that you hung from and the knife that was used to cut the rope, the blade was without a sharp edge so I had to use it like a saw which led to it fracturing" seeing John about to tear up Samuel pulled him close "You were always my friend regardless of your skin color and you still are" John let a few tear roll down his checks as he heard a gunshot.

"How dare you be friends with that coon they're only good for chaos! They need to be plagued from the earth!" screamed the young butcher who was standing in the door holding his father shot gun "I knew something was up when you wouldn't let me kill him" holding onto Samuel as he died John felt an wave of sorrow engulf him as it begin to mix with guilt John knew he could only blame himself for what just happened if only Samuel wouldn't have cut him down or greeted him so kindly he'd still be living. "You got to go coon your kind isn't welcome around here! One is too many and we all know what would happen if more was to come!" using all the strength he had left Samuel whispered into John's ear giving him one final piece of advice.

"Vengeance isn't the path to restore love"

"I understand Samuel now rest with God and sleep peacefully" John slowly brought Samuel to the ground using the butcher shop wall to prop him up "I'll keep your kindness in mind" drifting off to an eternal slumber Samuel had came to peace with the fact he was killed for being kind to everyone no matter who they were and in his spirit he truly believe once his eyes closed that John was going to kill his son for his own actions.

"Kendall you did wrong son…. Hell will welcome you" Speaking his final words Samuel died from the fatal gunshot he received from his son.

"You made me kill my father!" Screamed Kendall flexing his trigger finger firing at John who was knelt down in front of Samuel

"Kendall you killed your father the only man to ever showed me kindness and for that you will pay" placing his hand in front of Samuel's face John first moved it up then down followed by left then right "My the father, son and holy ghost guide you to a peaceful heaven Amen"

"You can't pray over him God doesn't hear prayers from your kind of people!" Firing another shot at John who paid him no mind Kendall moved closer "Next one goes in your head"

"Where have I heard that one before? Let me think" John stood up turning to face Kendall who used the handle of the shotgun to bludgeon him in the face breaking his nose "Slick shot kid"

"You will die again only Jesus is able to rise...You aren't him!" hearing his own words Kendall stood completely still having just noticed what his father had been telling him for years however it was too late for him. His action had already determined what would happen to him after death though it wasn't something he wanted to happen Kendall knew this altercation would be his last and it was his own fault. "It's me or you Harkness and I don't plan to die"

"First you talk about what people say in regards to more than one African American around then you claim god doesn't hear prayers from my kind which I'm assuming you're referring to that fact I'm Black what else could it be" Smiling as he placed his forehead into the shotgun Kendall was holding John continued "You claim we are only good for Chaos and That God needs to plague us from the Earth let's not forget the most recent bits. You called me an inexcusable slur more than once said my kind wasn't welcome you even went as fair to exclaim one of us it to many. Which leads to my all time favorite you think you know what would happen if more African American moved into town"

"I am right about everything I say and I standby it just like Pastor Aerius taught me! You want to play all tough this makes me shot easier Harkness!"

"There you go again with doing the same dumb shit" gripping Kendall's hand holding it on the trigger John used his strength to forcefully press on Kendall's fingers pulling the trigger sending a bullet through his own skull. "Do you understand now?"

"You should be dead" mumbled Kendall as he seen a single strain of blood trail down John's face from an open bullet wound that you could see completely through "That should of killed you and finally rid this town of their vermin"

"Nothing is going to change what Pastor Aerius has drilled in your head so I'm just going to have to kill you" grabbing Kendall by his shirt John threw him into the street just as a Horse and wagon pulled up in front of the butcher shop. "Let's get a few things cleared up before you die shell we" failing to see around the rowdy and unsteady horses that hauled the wagon John let revenge once again fuel him. As he felt his body surge he tore one of the wheels off the wagon having one side drop to the ground with an impactful force breaking the lock that allowed the occupants to exit trapping them inside. Handling the wheel with only his left hand having it in his palm John swung back ready to launch the wheel with all his might when he let go it went spiraling in a circle fast enough that it severed both horses' heads off and crashed right into the ground in front of Kendall stopping him in his tracks.

"There's nothing you can say to change my mind, you aren't anything but an unwanted pigmentation abomination that needs to be cleansed from Earth!" Kendall screamed out loud having to project his voice in order for John to hear it over all the panicking that was coming from the wagon's occupants. "Aerius had taught us all the correct ways on how to live!" screamed Kendall louder than before wanting to be heard "Pastor has made the greatest sacrifice for God's true vision of the human race and Earth, Not only did he make it once but he was forced to make it again when you killed Estelle!"

"Kendall you will never seen past Aerius's blinders and forever be lost on how this world truly works" John remarked as he punched his way into the wagon door ripping it off the hinges "Now you three need to get out of my site before you're killed" The occupants of the wagon jumped out and took off towards the sheriff's office.

"Harkness it's about time you owned up to your crimes and take responsibility for killing Estelle!" Bellowed Kendall as he patted his waist for his butcher's blade until he remembered he gave it to his father. Looking over at John who was still somewhat blocked by the wagon Kendall saw his blade stabbed into the door frame of the butcher shop and started to make a mental plan on how to retrieve it so he can protect himself again John.

"You have no right to say her name" Leaping over the wagon John saw Kendall dart back towards the butcher shop "I never killed her but I'm going to kill you!" Echoed John his voice radiating throughout the wind "I'd still prefer you to learn before you go to hell"

"I have nothing to learn from you! All darkies do is spin webs of lies!" trying to pull his blade from the wooden frame Kendall stumbled back just as it gave way slicing the throat of the sheriff who ran as fast as he could to assist once he was given the word that two men are having a brawl out in the streets. "Abraham I'm so sorry" trying to speak as his throat filled with blood Sheriff Abraham could only say a few words

"Sorry… he should….Don't cry… I came to help you…Only" choking on his own blood from the deep throat slitting he received on accident Sheriff Abraham die just because he came to help and assist having strong values in upholding the law.

"First your father now the Sheriff You seem to kill everyone who's trying to help you" applauding Kendall's actions towards accidently murdering the sheriff John took his chance to move closure coming face to face with Kendall who was standing with his blade one hand and shot gun in the other.

"Everyone seems to die when you came around but you're still living how's that far?" chucking the gun into the road Kendall dropped to his knees "Lord in heaven hear thy plea give me the strength needed to kill this demon of Lucifer who plagues the earth leaving death and darkness everywhere he goes"

"You won't get the strength you need after everything you proclaimed to me and your actions here today" picking up the gun that was thrown in the street John aimed it at Kendall's chest "I am not a plague and neither are others like me! We bring culture and joy! God loves us just like he loves you!" taking a few steps closure Kendall looked down the barrow of his own shotgun and saw nothing but darkness void of light "My pigmentation doesn't need to be cleansed from Earth…. I am Earth…Have you not seen how much black people match the nature of this planet? Apparently not if you think we are the abomination!"

"Pastor Aerius could not have been wrong!" Kendall screamed his eyes filled with tears as he looked at John. "He had a grand plan for us all to follow; he said it was God's plan! Pastor Aerius could not have been wrong!"

"Pastor Aerius has been wrong ever since Gunslingers stormed through town killing his youngest son" Thinking about that event made John's spine quiver he hadn't thought about the day Lawton was scalp and beheaded in years. The first Sunday of spring had just begin and the birds were chirping away the town wasn't relatively small but it wasn't no big city it had a bank, sheriff's office with jail cell, doctor's office, butcher shop, school house, smithy, many homes and the towns prize building the church who governed the towns laws. As Pastor Aerius was preaching a sermon about being kind to others in all paths of life a gang of Gunslingers stormed into town robbing the bank and starting a shoot out with the local Indian natives. One of the gunslinger's found himself being chased by Natives who wanted to kill him they chased him all the way to Pastor Aerius's home. One of the natives threw a tomahawk at the door getting it stuck into the wood just as the gunslinger closed it, while he was inside more natives on horseback stomped outside the house. They were ready to wait until the gunslinger got tired thinking if he's asleep he can't reach his pistol.

What they didn't consider when crafting this plan was that people my live in the house and that they could be home that very minute all the Natives had on their mind was kill the Gunslinger. The front door opened up and the young man gasped seeing the tomahawk he hadn't been feeling well so he didn't go with his family to church that morning however he wanted to enjoy the weather so he gathered his strength to walk out to the porch. The Natives were ready to retaliate against the Gunslinger for his action once he leaf the house he was hiding in, they captured the first person to walk out the front door using a net and dragged it the center of town for everyone to see.

Church was just getting out and Pastor Aerius came face to face with a Native covered by chalky warrior paint who explained the Natives tribe were about to make a human sacrifice. All the church goers didn't move from the church at all they could only watch in disbelief as one of their own was scalped and there was nothing they could do about it. As the Natives begun scalping the church attendees, Pastor Aerius and his wife who was over the moon for him at the time could see who it was the Natives had. Just as the last bit of his scalp was removed Pastor Aerius's wife screamed in terror seeing her baby boy that way it wasn't until the Natives used a sharp blade to remove his head did it seem like a tiny bit of Pastor Aerius died. That day had almost been gone for John's memory until Kendall said that the Pastor sacrificed for God's truest vision and then sacrificed again because his daughter is dead.

"Pastor had 3 children?" asked Kendall with confusion

"Yes and sadly the good ones are dead" remarked John lowering the shot gun he had aimed at Kendall feeling sorry for him. "I never learned the eldest son's name I just know he saw the world just like you do because of his father"

"Is how I see the world truly wrong?" cried Kendall throwing his hands to the sky

"You still have time to change and learn to teach others how to be better" softly stepping closer John wanted to take the blade that sat in front of Kendall on the ground

"You don't get it because you don't remember me" said a Chocked up Kendall

"I get you can do better and grow from what you have done Aerius can't control your mind all the time" remarked John as he lifted his foot moving it slowly towards Kendall

"Abraham and I were the ones who dragged you from your shop and whipped you all because Pastor Aerius said it was part of God's plan"

"You still have time to change Kendall" remarked John trying to reach for the blade Kendall had in front of him without being seen

"I hope you find what you're looking for Harkness…. I mean John" swiftly grabbing the blade Kendall slit his throat spraying John who had hit the concrete hard missing it as he lunged for Kendall's blade coming up short.

"In the end you choose violence and peace hopefully I can find a commend ground" grabbing for the blade John wiped the blood off using Kendall's shirt and placed the blade right with the gun he took from Waylon. "You were involved in Estelle's murder but kept it secret and for that I'm glad you're dying" holding the slit in his throat with both his hands Kendall only looked at John "Only those involved called me Harkness and I know each one of ya'll personally" jabbing the blade into Kendall's stomach John pulled up leaving a giant gash all the way up to neck. "I have a Pastor's son to kill for what he's done" cleaning the blade once again John walked towards the church he figured either the eldest son or the Pastor was going to be there, either way he would get to kill someone for what happened. As John got closer to the church he could hear prayers being taught and the man's voice was just who he expected it was Pastor Aerius himself.

Chapter 3: Prayers and Blood Jewels

"You must be lost because you aren't welcome here" remarked a deep voice from above John's head which caused him to turn and see a broad shoulder slender built man sitting on horseback. "I didn't stutter you lost?"

"I'm looking for Pastor Aerius" calmly said John trying not to make eye contact with the man on horseback.

"You must be a believer in God and want the good word of the pastor in your life" The man dismounted his horse but kept his hand on the reins so he could walk the horse next to him. "Sorry about that whole you aren't welcome here I thought you meant harm"

"Everyone thinks that about me when they first see me" the man took the reins tying them around a post that way his horse wouldn't ride off when he walked the rest of the way to Church with John. "I've had that reaction from people my whole life ain't nothing new"

"Well let's try and look on the bright side of this my new friend" as the two walked John begun to feel eerie it was as if he could sense what was about to happen. "I'm Ambrose by the way I help out around here a lot"

"Everyone calls me John I'm the local black smith"

"Local black smith you say?" Ambrose stopped and put his arm around John's shoulders "You must be New the last one died" taking his arm from around John's shoulder Ambrose noticed what kind of condition John was in from the torn clothing to the blood that soaked his clothing to the dirt and mud that was caked on his shoes and pants. "You've must have been through a lot"

"My life has had its up and downs it could be better" trying to keep a none suspicious distance from Ambrose and still maintain his ploy that he was the new black smith here to replace the old one was about to get more challenging. Everyone was walking out of the church after the final sermon right passed Ambrose and right passed John too it was as though they weren't visible to anyone but in reality the church goers just didn't care none of them liked Ambrose because of what he did so they just assumed John was with him so they paid no attention to him either. "Do they not see us at all?"

"They just don't like the fact I helped kill our last blacksmith for the crime he committed" stopping at the church doors and opening them Ambrose took one last look at John "They didn't like him but they liked what he could do"

"What was his crime?" curious about what is being said about him John wanted to stretch this as far has he could to gain information that he didn't have

"He fell in love with Estelle the Pastor's daughter and that cost him"

"Why'd that cost him?" John leaned closure to Ambrose making sure he was able to hear everything clearly

"When he fell in love with her he ruined her for all other men then he killed her" grabbing bibles off the pews and stacking them nicely on the alter Ambrose looked at John trying to figure out where he knew him from

"So love ruined her and he did what?" John started to grab bibles and help clean up hoping the distraction would be a good change of pace

"I swear you must be deaf or you're just nosey" chuckled Ambrose "I'll tell you just help me lift these pews they need to use this space when their isn't church for schooling right now until we can build a second school house"

"So love ruined her and he did what?" John wanted to know how they see him loving Estelle as ruining her

"He killed her and we killed him for it" Ambrose smiled thinking about what he did to help kill the old blacksmith even though he was talking to John.

"How'd he ruin her though was it just that fact he killed her?" lifting the last pew with Ambrose's help John noticed he had a gold cross necklace around his neck the same gold cross necklace he had given Estelle when she told him the news.

"He talked her into sleeping with him and deflowered her" ready to punch the wall Ambrose stopped touched the cross around his neck and took a breath

"So he was her first then killed her?"

"You sure do ask a lot of questions for someone new" Ambrose sat down on one of the pews that he and John just moved and started rubbing the cross necklace. "The Blacksmith fell in love with the Pastor's Daughter her name was Estelle and for some reason she fell in love with him too" taking a deep breath after saying that it looked as though Ambrose had just drank fire from an active volcano. "Rumor has it they had planned to run away together but around here we don't take lightly to races mixing especially when it comes to marriage and starting families" John sat listening he wanted to know everything that people had said or what rumors they were coming up with. "So when we discovered that she had given her innocent to that negro blacksmith we had to take a stand"

"So you killed a man over love and sex?" asked John

"No we killed a man for loving someone he shouldn't and destroying her for any respectable white man her father would see fit for her to marry"

"That doesn't seem to be far or even lawful to murder someone over"

"So you see that as fine?" Ambrose turned his head towards John waiting for his response

"It doesn't matter who you love as long as everyone is happy" Ambrose threw a punch striking John in the mouth

"You'll end up just like the last blacksmith with seeing the world like that" John started laughing at Ambrose "What's so funny?"

"You said I'd end up like the last blacksmith"

"Damn straight you will"

"So does that mean I have to deflower and knock up your dead sister like he did?" lunging at John trying to wrestle him to the ground Ambrose was filled by rage

"I never said she was Pregnant or my sister!" grunted Ambrose

"Guess this game is over time to come clean" Ambrose started Punching John in his face until blood appeared on his knuckles

"How'd you know those things?" laughing through a bloody mouth John spit a mouth full of blood to the right of his face getting it down his check and ear

"You said I'd end up like the old blacksmith" pushing Ambrose off him John got to his foot "I am the old Blacksmith the one you killed"

"John as in John Harkness?" asked Ambrose

"In the flesh and here for vengeance" said John mimicking a fake bow trying to be sarcastic

"I'm not the guy you're looking for I didn't do anything wrong" said Ambrose wiping John's blood off his knuckles

"Not the guy? You just said you helped kill me!"

"You didn't die from what I did it was the others who killed you"

"What did you do Ambrose?" grabbing him by the throat John started to choke Ambrose "What did you do?"

"I'll never tell you I will take it to my grave"

"That's going to be sooner than you thought" As the two kept fighting John noticed that even though he had been stronger than Waylon and Kendall this fight with Ambrose was going to be a match for him. "You did the worse thing of all if you are going to stay quite about it"

"You'll have to catch me to kill me" running out of the church darting for his horse Ambrose wanted to get as far away from John as he could

"I'll catch you and kill you Ambrose!" running after the horse Ambrose was riding John gave into the vengeance that brewed in his heart and caught up to the horse.

"Someone's learned a new trick well so did I" Keeping an eye on John's speed Ambrose pulled out a lasso and looped him by his neck throwing his speed off sending him crashing to the ground being dragged behind the horse by his neck. "You should be fond of this by now what's this the 2nd time you're going to be hung?" charging for nearby trees Ambrose smiled feeling the wind brush up against his skin, the only thought going through his mind was why he hadn't recognized John before they entered the church.

"Ambrose my boy what have you got their?" screamed Pastor Aerius beading the rosary he had wrapped around his right wrist that normally draped down his palm. Pulling the reins on his horse after hearing the screams Ambrose felt the rope in his hand tighten as John tumbled his body maintaining the speed the horse was running "You can't hang anyone without a trail my boy"

"Father that is John Harkness" keeping a straight face Pastor Aerius looked over at John who had crashed into the large red oak tree that was only a few inches away from where Ambrose halted his horse. Noticing how bloody the back of John's head was the only thoughts on Pastor Aerius's mind was that hitting the tree at that speed most definitely had to cause injury or worse death. He didn't want to believe what Ambrose was screaming about and it helped not seeing the face that belonged to the man he was looking at, to him the man was just a random black man his son was attempting to hang out in public.

"That can't be John Harkness he is dead, you must have mistook another due to your regret" said Pastor Aerius as he walked over brushing his hand over the two deep scarlet lines that intersected on the horse's hind end. He remembered the day Ambrose road the horse to church its glistening white coat caked in blood from the body that had been thrown over it. "Such a mighty stallion you tamed it came in handy"

"Father that man is John Harkness" demanded Ambrose has he pointed toward the red oak

"John was badly murdered my son along with my beloved daughter" wiping a tear from his eye Pastor Aerius wouldn't looked at anyone he just looked at the ground "They are both with God now"

"That man is JOHN HARKNESS!" anger escaped with his tone proving just how much Ambrose felt disrespected over the fact he wasn't being taken serious

"I watched him get hanged myself boy do not take that tone with me" breaking his gaze at the ground Pastor Aerius walked to Ambrose until they were eye to eye "You of all people should know"

"I know the wicked things YOU had me do and they haunt me" murmured Ambrose through weeping words. He was trying to be brave enough to stand up to Pastor Aerius but felt the Pastor's pull and how much control it had over him.

"It was for the better of the people!" blurted pastor Aerius as he threw his hands in the air "Lord up above allow your earthly child Ambrose to know his sins will be repented and he has been resolved for them"

"My sins?" sarcastically remarked Ambrose dropping the rope that was still wrapped around John's neck. When John hit the red oak he was knocked unconscious due to his skull shattering sending bone shards into his brain.

"Murder is a sin that stains the heart of the murderer and only our lord can forgive you for it" Pastor Aerius trailed his eyes along the trail of blood leading to John that he hadn't noticed before "What you did was against the commandants and you must beg for forgiveness my son" reaching into the saddle bag that hung over his horse Ambrose drew a small cloth holding it in his hand. Wrapping his hands around it tightly he begin to cry "That's it cast those demons of regret away allow the holy ghost to touch your heart once again bringing you from the darkness" slamming his hand onto Ambrose's chest with a mighty force causing his let out a gasp for air Pastor Aerius started speaking "Miserere tui terreni prolis Ambrosii, Deus, Eleison! Ad Te spectat praesidium! Sub umbra alarum tuarum deduci vult, donec periculum transit"

"These aren't my demons!" Yelled Ambrose tightening his grip on the cloth he took from his bag "These aren't my demons!"

"Ambrose my son you brought these demons into your soul when thou killed" breaking free when Pastor Aerius's praying he felt great not having pressure on his chest "You know what you did and so does God"

"I was only following an order given to me" turning to look away Ambrose felt hands on his shoulder's firmly gripping them "Do not touch me father, I have always honored you, I would like the same respect"

"Pater mi, defende et serva Ambrosium ab impugnationibus impiorum et invisibilium daemonum in Iesu nomine!" with each word he spoke Pastor Aerius dug his nails deeper into Ambrose's shoulders

"God does not have to forgive me!" taking the pain being inflicted unto him Ambrose could sense he was being filled with courage to stand up to his father.

"Beg our savoir for forgiveness!" yelled Pastor Aerius he could no longer hold back his feelings about how Ambrose was acting and let out his growing anger.

"BEG!" clenching the cloth in one hand Ambrose made the other into a fist spinning punching Pastor Aerius in the jaw "YOU WANT ME TO BEG!" sending another fist connecting to the same spot Ambrose shoved the cloth at Pastor Aerius "YOU SHOULD BE BEGGING FATHER!"

"I have no reason to beg Our lord for forgiveness" lifting his hands palms out Pastor Aerius let the cloth drop to the ground where it made a loud thud when hitting the dirt "What is in that cloth?"

"That cloth is your sin father" laughing as he kicked the cloth with his foot revealing the pistol that was wrapped in it. "That's your pistol isn't it?"

"Am...Ambrose that's not the pistol..."

"Used to murder Estelle? Of course it is I kept it" feeling the blood drain from his face Pastor Aerius was left pale and petrified "I felt you'd want the pistol back that holster looked empty" leaning down making sure he grabbed the pistol by the cloth it was wrapped in Ambrose placed it into Pastor Aerius's hands "This is your sin and only your sin" smiling as he watched the cloth drop to the ground Ambrose was overcome with joy when Pastor Aerius stood holding the pistol "Beg God for forgiveness over your actions father" as he take a step to the left Ambrose leaned in and whispered "These demons are yours and Estelle's death is on your hands" still standing petrified by what was happening Pastor Aerius slowly ran his fingers along the pistol's barrel.

"My pistol was used to kill my little girl?" opening the chamber seeing only one bullet left Pastor Aerius pointed it at Ambrose "Beg our lord for forgiveness on earth or you can beg him in person!" fighting his words due to crying Pastor Aerius felt he didn't have any more options.

"You don't have the balls to pull that trigger you couldn't hurt a soul"

"I'll do what must be done God will forgive me"

"Father!" bellowed Ambrose walking closer to the pistol "You claim I have sinned and demons have claimed my mortal soul over my actions" touching his forehead to the barrel "You preach that I must ask God nee Beg God for forgiveness!" taking a deep breath as he smirked "You fail to see that it was you that gave the order and it was your pistol that was used. I regret my actions and I feel remorse however my skin never touch that pistol's steel"

"What does that have to do with it? You are a murderer" remarked Pastor Aerius as he moved his finger closer to the trigger just hovering it slightly above.

"YOU MADE ME A MURDERER!" shouted Ambrose sending spit flying out his mouth "YOU SENT ME TO KILL ESTELLE... YOUR OWN DAUGHTER! SHE WAS MY SISTER! DO YOU FAIL TO REMEMBER THAT TOO?" continuing to shout everything that he had harbored deep inside Ambrose knew someone was dying over this argument.

"She had to die for loving that man"

"You sent me to kill your own daughter just because she loved someone you didn't agree with"

"You are acting like others don't do this to keep their family pure" pulling the trigger only to find out it was jammed Pastor Aerius smacked Ambrose a crossed the face with the barrel. "I sent you to kill her of course but I wasn't the one to pull the trigger you were"

"I own up to my actions, you use our lord to justice what you did"

"You were all I had left Ambrose! Your mother turned his back, your brother was murdered and your sister fell in love with him" pointing over to John who was slowly coming to "I knew who that was when I looked over this town only had one coon"

"Father, what are you going to do?" holding his face as he spoke Ambrose had lost the courage that had entered his heart

"I'm leaving you to finish him off" throwing the pistol at Ambrose's foot Pastor Aerius looked at his son "God knows everything and forgives" stepping around walking away from his son Pastor Aerius turned around "That gun you used the first bullet killed your mother" pulling himself together and standing up Ambrose pulled on his gloves and picked up the pistol.

"I have to be the one to kill John it's what God would want" grabbing the rope yanking it to him pulling a groggy John towards him "You won't be able to heal from this" firing the pistol's last bullet Ambrose watched as brain chunks sprayed out the back of John's skull sending him to his knees. "Harkness this is your final stand"

"You never fired the first shot that day did you?" trying to see past the blood draining down his face John glared at Ambrose "You fired on Estelle but your shot didn't kill her she was already dead"

"You must die!" throwing the loose end of the rope around John's neck for tighter support Ambrose threw what he had left in his hand over a tree branch hoisting John off the ground hanging him. "To think I didn't recognize you"

"I am going to kill you" uttered John as his eyes rolled in the back of his head and his body stopped trying to break lose.

"I can now sleep in peace John Harkness had finally been put to rest" mounting his horse and riding off Ambrose removed the gold cross he wear dropping it on the ground. Believing he had found away to kill John Harkness it didn't take long for Ambrose to ride to the church and tell Pastor Aerius what had taken place. "Father hanging him and shooting him in the head worked"

"You have accomplished the unthinkable my son and for that you must be rewarded" drawing a twisted blade covered in satanic marking Pastor Aerius stabbed Ambrose right in the abdomen turning the blade. "Our Lord's bible didn't have all the answers but I found what I needed" dropping to his knees blooding out Ambrose's final thought was something john had said.

"Was John right? Was Estelle dead before you sent me?"

"Leave it to Harkness to discover what really happened. Of course she was dead" Pastor Aerius's face distorted and his smile curled at the end of his mouth "I killed Estelle!"

Chapter 4: Sow

As he hung John's spirit lost all hope for vengeance he was ready to cross over to the afterlife and greet Estelle. He felt as though he was failure believing he was brought back for nothing since he couldn't even seem to keep himself out of harms ways. There wasn't much left to do he had proven he couldn't beat Ambrose and if he couldn't beat him how was he able to face Pastor Aerius and kill him. Those thoughts raced over and over inside of John's head as he hung silently feeling the sun's warmth dissipate around him leaving only the frozen bite of winter air "Wake your ass up" said a woman as she smacked John on his foot spinning him "You really about to give in? Didn't think they'd win" shaking her head in visible disappointment the woman looked up at John who was struggling to open his eyes having them covered in dried blood.

"Who are you?" John said struggling to breathe between words since the nuce around his neck was tied tighter than it was during his first hanging.

"I'm the woman who saves your ass" grabbing John by his calf the woman closed her eyes seeing what had happened so far and determining how much fight was left in John. She didn't know the connection worked both ways so while she saw what John had done since he returned from the dead, John was able to see the woman's life and why she was helping him. He was able to see that she was just a conduit for the spirit of the crow which had taken control of the only person who had faced the same backlash as him. It was the crow spirit that not only brought him back from the dead but also allowed the woman to stand her ground against everyone in town when their hatred turned to her. The crow spirit knew it would require a familiar face when it came time to resurrect John and by helping an innocent bar maiden take charge of her life standing up to everyone who tried to test her. She allowed the crow to use her body when it needed to assist John. Unlike John she wasn't granted any power the only change that accrued was she started to fight back and stopped taking shit from those who resented her just because she was black in a town of many white families.

"You brought me back?" placing his hands around the rope John pulled it far enough away from his throat in order to speak without all the pressure "You did this to me, Why?" he questioned feeling the tightness of the nuce press against his fingers pushing them against his neck catching him of guard causing him to let out a gasp for air.

"I liked Estelle she wasn't her family" jumping up snapping the tree branch using her bare hands the woman gracefully landed back on the ground where John dropped hard. "They blamed you and took her life. You love her so you must seek revenge" Knowing that she could see into John's life the woman grabbed his hand flooding his mind with every memory he made with Estelle and reminding him how much he truly loved her. Feeling his love for Estelle grow inside his heart John felt like he could take on anyone he wanted to bring her to peace. As that love he had for Estelle grew John started to feel an intense love for someone he had never met, this person was the woman's husband who had passed away peacefully. She never stopped loving him and longed to be by his side each day when the town folks belittled her or treated her like trash it was the love she carried for him that kept her fighting. This love was now unknowingly being mirrored into John who could feel how much sorrow the woman carried being separated from the love of her life and why she allowed the crow spirit to help her. When the crow first visited her all it did was call loudly and fly away the woman didn't noticed something was going on until the crow perched itself onto her shoulder without making a sound. Gesturing for it to guide her the woman followed the crow as it flew into the graveyard landing on her husband's tombstone, as her eyes filled with tears remember how much she loved him the woman noticed John and Estelle for the first time. They were cuddling in the shade of the mighty oak tree that grew on the hill top she could see how much they were in love but knew trouble would come once people found out since in their town it was frowned upon for a white girl to be involved with a black man. The crow that guided her to the graveyard gazed into her eyes showing her what fate would be bestowed upon John. That was when she decided to open her soul to the crow spirit vowing once John returned the spirit would be able to pilot her body keeping him on the right path.

"All I crave is vengeance" John said while he untied the rope from his throat placing it around his waist "This is for Ambrose when I see him again"

"Vengeance or Revenge your black ass still here talking to me and not out there" pulling a metal flask from her ash leather coat pocket the woman swilled every drop that was contained inside "I'll keep an eye out for you but you need to stop taking on so many deadly injuries"

"I can't control how they try to kill me again" remarked John

"Weak ass already claiming he will die, Thought you were a fighter" snuffed the woman tapped the bottom of her flash trying to get every drop

"I am a fighter and I will prove it by getting my vengeance" John said with a confident tone banging his balled fist upon his chest trying to prove he was ready

"If I have to see you one more time I might just kill you myself" the woman said putting her flash back into her coat and pulling out a full bottle of liquor using her teeth to pop off the top.

"I can't control if they try to kill me again" softly said John keeping his head trying not to make eye contact

"Bitch you better!" the woman responded quickly before disappearing leaving only the reflection a set of wings flapping.

"How do you aspect me to do that!" John screamed into thin air noticing the woman had disappeared. "I need to find Ambrose he's first on my vengeance list" walking past a horse trough John caught his reflection seeing how he looked after being drugged through the dirt and blooding the whole time. "This bullet hole should have healed" poking at the open wound in the center of his forehead John started to second guess the fact he could heal from anything. Listening closely to his surrendering John could tell there was a river and possible waterfall close by and he walked towards them. "Finally I can feel alive again" said John as he undressed and stepped into the river using his hand to peel away dried dirt and blood.

"You don't belong in that river it belongs to the fish" bellowed a native man who was lurking from the trees. The man's skin was bronze and he had braided hair the reach down to his knees though it was infested by what looked like a small nest of black widow spiders. His clothing was just clothes layered over top each other. He had waves tattooed onto his left bicep and had his bow wrapped around his shoulder and torso.

"I don't need this I just need to be cleaned" keeping his head on a swivel John could feel the vengeance in his heart becoming his driving factor. He was ready to take vengeance out on anyone who crossed him.

"You're bathing in that river!" the voice screeched "You are disturbing nature and that river belongs to the fish" tracking the water with his eyes John shoved his hand quickly into the river grabbing a salmon holding it up to the woods so that his stalker could watch what he was about to do.

"You mean this fish?" tiring into the raw fish John sensed his life was in danger tilting his head just in time missing an arrow that was shot at him hearing it land inside a tree breaking off the bark

"Get out of the river!" demanded the Native man who hand another arrow pulled back aiming for John

"Claim down I will when I am done" applying pressure trying to get the mud off his arms John couldn't focus on cleaning him when he had a native screaming at him over a river bank.

"You will now!" echoed the Native man as he shot another arrow at john who again instinctively moved out the way. "You will exit the river I will not miss again" remarked the Native who was still using the trees as coverage

"Listen you really don't want any part of this" John attempted to warn everyone who he came in contact with after coming back from the dead. His tolerance for their prejudice had weighted thin to the point he didn't have any it was kill first ask why later.

"I've killed your kind before" pulling back their bow the native sent a third arrow at John who caught it out of the air "How did you do that?" coming from his hiding spot with astonishment coating his face the Native couldn't understand how that was possible. The man he was trying to remove from the river had dodged twice of his arrows and was able to catch the third with his bare hands.

"I'm special so if you don't mind I would like to finish bathing" as he finished washing what he could John turned to see the Native lurking at him mere feet away from the river bank

"You don't seem to fit nature, you smell like blood and rotten flesh" reaching for his filthy clothing that he had placed on a large rock John was met with an arrow to the neck. The Arrow wasn't fired from a bow it was forcefully thrust into John's neck at close range by the Native who used his bare hands. The impact only cut a small incision however as the arrow head pierced John's skin he felt his thrist for vengeance spike.

"I am Natok and my tribe was native to this town. We were forced off our land and dwell near the river now" Natok was shocked when he offered his hand to John and it was smacked away. John didn't want help out of the river he was capable of doing everything himself. He also didn't want help from someone who tried to shot him with three arrows and stabbed him with a fourth.

"I'm invading your space I get it" John walked out the river placing his clothing back on and walked away. Natok used one of his arrows to grab onto John's shirt twisting his arrow head around the fabric yanking him close.

"You'll stay and feast with my tribe tonight" said Natok as he reached for another arrow stabbing it straight down into John's shoulder. Using the arrow entangled in John's shirt Natok started to pull him away from the river. When he saw it was going to be difficult he gripped the arrow he stabbed into John's shoulder and choices to pull him through the river hoping the uneasy current would help in his benefit "Just don't lose your head tonight"

"I don't plan on losing my head or going to a feast" said John as his anger grew into a vengeful fury. He didn't have time to play guest to a bunch of Indians no matter how many arrows Natok stabbed into him. He wanted to get back to hunting down Ambrose but couldn't due to Natok. Using both arrows to thrash John into the river Natok quickly placed his knee onto John's chest keeping him submerged under water until the air bubbles coming to the surface are tiny.

"Do you understand you don't have a say you will be coming with me" disclosed Natok who was fed up with John fighting him. Letting him up from underneath the river Natok witnessed John's lips turn from a milky grey back to their natural color but the discoloration around his eyes stayed.

"Once I'm not being pupated by your arrows I'm going to kill you" exclaimed John once he got his first breath after being held under water. Having his grip tight on the arrow Natok dragged a weakened John through the river to the other side where he was greeted by more member of his tribe.

"He's feisty but I have weakened him, He will make for an excellent guest at our feast tonight" said Natok to the other members of his tribe

"Natok this man smells like rotten flesh I don't believe he will do" remarked a younger native as leaned down and sniffed John "The tribe hasn't has a guest at our feast for months and you bring this" the same younger native pointed at John trying to indicate to Natok who he was talking about

"Atrok'n this feast will be our greatest yet can you recall the last time our tribe feasted on Wasicu Hawiya?" as a smile grew on Atrok'n's face he opened his mouth to show each tooth had been shaved down to be sharp. Trying to rise to his feet John was yanked back down each time by the arrow in his shoulder

"He doesn't look Wasicu but I agree it's been to long we haven't had Hawiya in any form from many moons. Most our tribe is eating dried fruits, nuts and what vegetables that will grow" looking at John

Atrok'n licked his lips and rubbed his stomach "You are Wasicu Hawiya aren't you excited to be the guest at our feast tonight?" Atrok'n asked John as he squeezed didn't muscles on John's body

"Get off of me!" demanded John as he made two fists swinging them into the air trying to hit someone "I am not Hawiya!" exclaimed John ripping his shirt causing the arrow that was twisted into to drop to the ground

"Natok get him!" yelled Atrok'n in a panic he didn't know how to handle John's attitude and was frightened "He's going to ruin the feast if you don't do something Natok!" Atrok'n moved away from John just as he started to rise to his feet.

"Get back down on the ground where you belong" Natok grabbed the arrow in John's shoulder and tired to pull him back down to the ground only to find that John didn't feel the pain anymore and he wasn't going down easy.

"I told you I don't going to a feast yet alone being the main dish!" proclaimed John as he ripped the arrow from his shoulder throwing it down. "Which one of you wants to die first?"

"I'll take you Pale face" said a deep toned native as he walked up behind Atrok'n. He was the only other native at the river and he was the scariest. Standing at a mighty 6 feet 4inches covered in scars with war paint coating his face he was a force of nature "When I'm done with you becoming Wasicu Hawiya will be the least of your worries"

"I have to warn you I'm out for vengeance and you're standing in my way" said John as he looked the Native up and down "You'll just fall faster if you don't back out now"

"Back out? You must have lost too much blood. Today is your last day to breath pale face" looking at John the Native clapped his hands together "Let's get this started" slapping his overly large hands over top John's shoulder arrow the Native was able to induce pain causing John to scream out loud "You are fun to hurt"

"Tenderize the Wasicu Hawiya for us Moni'ta'ee" excitedly yelled Atrok'n as he begun to jump around expressing his joy. John could tell if he didn't figure out a strategy he wouldn't win against Moni'ta'ee and he'd have to face the woman who warned him not to die.

"You've been warned and now I'll show you why you don't ever keep a man from his vengeance" jumping in the air punching Moni'ta'ee in the face John watched as the blow did nothing the Native just smiled. Taking a step back before trying to sweep the leg John wasn't sure how he could win this fight but he was going to do everything in his power to do so. Rapidly jabbing Monti'ta'ee's stomach building up speed John used his right hand attempting to swing a punch, just before his punch connected John dropped his right hand and used his left hand to uppercut Moni'ta'ee sending the native stumbling back.

"Natok I thought you and Atrok'n said this man was Wasicu Hawiya? He has the spirit of an Akicita I shall call him Akicita Hawiya. Bring the pot to a boil I am about to finish this" placing his whole hand around John's face lifting him in the air as he proceeded to squeeze Moni'ta'ee kept apply pressure until John was no longer kicking his legs trying to break free "It is over the Akicita Hawiya is lifeless time to boil it"

"I got the spices and vegetables" screeched Atrok'n not trying to hide his excitement. Natok had gotten a fire blazing under a large cauldron while Moni'ta'ee was taking care whatever life was still in John's body.

"Why wait for the others when we can feast upon the Wasicu Hawiya right now?" Natok asked Atrok'n who stopped was throwing handfuls of spices into the cauldron when he heard the question

"YES! YES! WE FEAST ON WASICU HAWIYA NOW" replied Atrok'n whose excitement was growing the closer it got to placing John into the boiling cauldron. Picking John's body up by his chin Natok spoke to him

"Now you'll know what it's like to be a helpless fish in a river and I'm the monster who will take a bite" letting go of John's chin watching his head drop on the ground with a thud Natok instructed Moni'ta'ee to lift the body and drop it in the cauldron. As he went to left John's body something didn't feel right there was a sharp pain in the back of Monti'ta'ee's neck causing him to drop John back on the ground. "What is wrong with you it doesn't take much to move an unconscious man" seeing Moni'ta'ee drop to his knees Natok noticed the shaft of a arrow sticking out of his neck meaning the arrow head was completely in his neck possibly against his spine.

"I did warn you" jumping behind Moni'ta'ee tying his own ponytail around his neck John pulled with all his might until only the sound of a spine snapping could be heard. "You're next Atrok'n after what you called me!" John was invigorated from playing possum and killing off the biggest of the three.

"Natok do something you promised me Wasicu Hawiya I'm starving Natok do something" panicking over what to do Atrok'n ran and hide behind the cauldron where John couldn't reach "You can't get me here I'm safe" nodding his head yes playing along John pulled the rope from around his waist refastened it into a nuce and looped it around Atrok'n's neck yanking him with enough force he was dragged right into the boiling cauldron screaming as he was boiled alive. Taking the rope from Atrok'n's neck John didn't feel any of the heat from the boiling water when he stuck his hand in. Afraid of what he saw Natok stopped a few paces from John and pulled a spear from behind a tree.

"Oh I'm so scared, that's one Natok" remarked John as he sized up the spear's dimensions

"I was not asking if you were!" attacking with his spear Natok was aiming for John's stomach "I will drag you into the cauldron myself"

"That's three my turn" said John as he cracked his knuckles

"You skipped two you must want to die quickly" said Natok as he lunged forward with his spear trying to impale John

"You right" sending a quick jab to Natok's jaw followed by a powerful upper cut that sent Natok to the ground "Theirs your two" John looked at the Natok and noticed that he looked familiar. "You scalped Aerius's Son"

"He and the gunslingers ravished my family and land" yelled an emotional Natok as he tried to hide that fact he was afraid about what might happen to him.

"You murdered an innocent kid for what?" asked John with a demanding tone, he wanted answers and it was about time he got them from someone.

"He was a murderous gun slinger!" screamed Natok has he climb to his feet. Kicking him back down using his right foot John pulled his gun on Natok aiming it at his face.

"He was an innocent kid you're the villain in his eyes" bellowed John he wanted to put Natok in his place and prove that actions make you who you are. "After what you, Atrok'n and Moni'ta'ee tried to do to here today that just proves you are the villain. I get trying to take me on but you scalped an innocent kid over mistaken identity"

"They all look identical so why does it matter" placing the gun back on his waist John extended his hand to Natok who slapped it away just like when he extended his hand to John over the other side of the river.

"You all die the same too" swiftly pulling the blade he kept during his fight with Kendall from his waist John made a cut a crossed Natok's forehead deep enough to force his fingers inside

"What are you doing?" Natok cried out in pain thrashing around trying to break free from John's hold

"Seems only fitting" using force John peeled off the top of Natok's head holding onto bloody flesh and hair. "You look better this way" toughing the top of Natok's skull over by Monti'ta'ee's corpse John felt as though he was gaining strength having just taken on three Natives who wanted to feast on him and defeating all of them.

"You have damned me to death you monster" looking at John through blood coated eyes Natok noticed he didn't move a step. "You have murdered three of a kind the rest of the Tribe will hunt you down for what you did hear today!" shouted Natok exerting the little energy he had left

"you sowed your fate when you shot that first arrow" drawing a handful of arrow from Natok's holder John shoved them all into the top of his skull "Native arrowhead now" Natok fell to the ground whispering one word that sent shivers down John's spine he didn't know how to interrupt what he had just heard

"Harkness…"whispered Natok as his face hit the ground.

Chapter 5: Prayer for your soul

    Looking at Ambrose's lifeless corpse Pastor Aerius know he needed to figure out a way to explain his son's disappearance to his followers. "I'll tell them you have left to preach the gospel of Christ to the east" dragging his son's body down into a cellar Pastor Aerius took a key from underneath his shirt. "You'll be okay here with your brother" as he threw Ambrose's body into a dimly lit room a small tear formed in his eyes seeing both his sons dead having their flesh rotting away. "You both should have respected the word of Christ where did I go wrong with raising you"

"You forced it down their throats Aerius!" remarked a woman

"That mouth of yours is what got you down here you disobedient wench" turning to face the woman who speak to him Pastor Aerius shinned a lantern on her face revealing the hatred in her eyes "How do your chains feel my love?"

"Like I'm shackled to a god who has no mercury for his people" spitting onto Aerius's face the woman thrashed her body loudly shaking her chains "Your own wife! Aerius you imprisoned your own wife!" screamed the woman as she continued to thrash "You're not worthy of your lords love!"

"I'm not worthy! How can you speak of worthiness when you blindly turned away!" striking his wife on her face Aerius locked eyes with her "I hate when I have to teach you a lesson"

"Teach a lesson? I'm not one of your followers I was your wife!"

"Yes my wife a woman of God a Beautiful woman of God until your heart turned to darkness" walking towards his dead boys kneeling down next to his youngest Aerius tilted the boy's rotting away face to him "This was the face of a boy who gave his soul to God only to find darkness clouded him and Satan tested him" dropping the boy's face watching as skin peeled off "His obsessions are what lead to his death and for that I feel responsible"

"YOU ARE RESPONSIBLE FOR ALL OF THIS AERIUS!" screamed the woman her eyes filling with tears "YOU MURDERED YOUR FAMILY WHEN THEY WERE STILL BREATHING BY FORCING YOUR VIEWS ABOUT CHRIST ONTO US ALL!" punching his wife in her stomach with all his might Aerius grabbed onto the cross he wore around his neck.

"Loquere Dominus huic mulieri et lucere lumen tuum super animam suam rebellem" leaning forward so that his wife could see his cross Aerius placed his hand onto her head "Ejice te ipsum daemonium dimitte hanc mulierem Christi anima eius est et illi soli ego te in eius nomine arguo" his wife stopped thrashing and did not move all she did was look at him with tears in her eyes seeing the man her husband had become.

"I am not possessed by a demon" she cried gashing for air coughing as tears poured down her cheeks

"That is the demon leaving you it is the blessing of our Lord" spoke Aerius softly as he wiped her tears away " I felt betrayed when you no longer join me in church Abigail" licking his fingers tasting his wife's tears Aerius grabbed her head stabling it licking the tears from her cheek up to your eyes kissing them gently "One day they will see The glory Jesus has to offer once again" cringing at her husband's touch Abigail attempted to break her hands free by shaking them violently she didn't want him to touch her at all and it disgusted her when he did.

"My cough is from crying so much not a demon and don't touch me" cried out Abigail

"You are my wife I will do what I choice with you, in the eyes of God you were put on this earth for me!" Angrily remarked Aerius as he took a stop back looking Abigail up and down "It's been so long since I've had your body my dear"

"I AM NOT PROPERTY AND DON'T THINK ABOUT IT!" striking Abigail with force Aerius scoffed at her flaring his nostrils to show he was displeased with her and angry. "I RESENT CHRIST FOR TAKING MY HUSBAND'S LOVE AWAY FROM ME!"

"I never stopped loving you, I just grew to love him more, He is my savior!" trying to keep claim Aerius took a step back from Abigail focusing his eyes onto the wooden cross he had nailed above her head

"I WAS YOUR WIFE YOU VOWED TO LOVE ME UNTIL THE END!"

"You are still my wife and my love for you never faltered" making the sign of the cross Aerius's eyes started to water "Why must you be this way Abigail? Why?"

"What a rage filled woman? Maybe because I've been chained up to a wall for almost a year! That might have something to do with it!" still moving her arms trying to free them hoping the chains had worn themselves down Abigail felt a small crack form on the chain she had on her right hand, the metal was sharp when it started to crack and nicked her palm as she finessed it out. "Finally I can reach for you!" said Abigail with excitement in her voice as she reached out grabbing Aerius by his long lushes hair pulling him close to her "Aerius you destroy everything you hold dear with that controlling attitude" feeling the products Aerius puts in his hair to make it lushes and straight Abigail let out a whale at the top of her lungs right into his ear. She hadn't noticed the cut on her palm until the product got into it and caused it to start burning.

"What is wrong with you woman?"

"You deserve to die!" remarked Abigail as she was forced to let go due to the burning being too intense

"When my lord calls me home I will happily go, not a day sooner so you need to watch that tongue"

"Oh I'm so scared what are you going to quote a bible verse" making a fist with her freed hand Abigail swung it at Aerius who had moved far enough away from her his work table was behind him "You're just like your brother you believe every word from that book!" swinging vigorously hoping she'd have enough lean on her body that she'd hit him Abigail's rage kept increasing.

"Don't you bring up my brother just because you can't see how amazing Jesus Christ is and how much he blesses his followers, My Lord lives in my heart and I'm becoming sick of your rebellious attitude" Turning to his work table scanning for one specific item Aerius moved quickly to Abigail once he found it "This should help you" splashing holy water onto Abigail believing it will cleanse her Aerius watched as the love his wife had for him left her eyes and it was replaced by hatred. He was running out of options to save her soul he thought and only had one last thought but it was barbaric and even he was scared to attempt it.

"After seeing what that book has done to you I'm glad Eliphaz shot himself when he thought the devil was going to claim his soul" hearing his brother's name infuriated Aerius causing him to let out his brewing anger and strike Abigail in her face. As his fist met the side of his wife's faces both heard breaking and Abigail started crying from the pain she couldn't even let out a scream she was so much in shock.

"Eliphaz was a man of God who started down a dark path, He was a great man" clasping his cross Aerius ran to get his bible he could feel he had wronged Jesus by striking his wife with that much force, letting anger taint your soul was a sin and by letting it out he showed Christ that his love could teeter. Grabbing his bible Aerius flipped it to *Ephesians 5:25-29* and begun reciting the passage "Husbands, love your wives, as Christ loved the Church and gave himself up her, that he might sanctify her, having cleansed her by the washing of water with the word, so that he might present the church to himself in splendor, without spot or wrinkle or any such thing, that she might be holy and without blemish. In the same way husbands should love their wives as their own bodies. He who loves his wife loves himself. For no one ever hated his own flesh, but nourishes and cherishes it, just as Christ does with the church"

"Eliphaz wasn't any man of God in his final days and you know it"

"Don't let that mouth speak lies" Abigail flinched when Aerius spoke she wanted to be heard and try to get through to him but now even his voice frightened her. "He was a pure man of God until he started talking with that woman she was the one who blinded him from the lord's shine"

"Kathryn didn't blind Eliphaz she believed in Christ and was more devoted than he was" leaning her head to the side Abigail was trying to ease the pain she felt. "That woman was the best thing to happen to your brother just like I was the best thing to happen to you"

"God was the best thing to happen to me!" remarked Aerius as he tightened his grip on his bible "He brought me you and we had 3 wonderful children that were devoted followers until you changed them"

"I didn't change them you were the one that killed Ambrose and let Estelle be murdered by that blacksmith" still fighting the pain in her mouth Abigail could fell she was getting tired from it but was afraid to go to sleep "You even stood by why Levi was scalped by that native, Some father you were" spitting at him again Abigail could feel her lips were drying out from not having anything to drink the only liquid that touched her lips were the tears she shed.

"They were not my children once they turned away from God"

"They weren't your children? Ambrose looked just like you did when we first meant and Estelle had your eyes" releasing what she just did had Abigail closing her eyes out of fear

"Neither is alive now! My sons are in that room rotting away and for my daughter" Aerius moved away from Abigail taking steps past his work table walking over to a thin curtain pulling it back showing Abigail what was behind it "As for my precious daughter her body is right here" looking over Aerius shoulder to see what he was talking about Abigail hoped she wouldn't see Estelle's dead body.

"You have her corpse like a trophy!"

"NO, I am trying to preserve her until my lord returns life to her as he did Lazarus" Aerius walked over to Estelle's corpse and ran his index finger down her cheek "My precious girl you will return to me one day"

"AERIUS YOU HAVE FUCKING LOST IT!" Abigail scream as loud as she could only being able to watch "YOU KEEP ME CAPTIVE AND HOARD THE DEAD BODIES OF YOUR KIDS!"

"If only you were like them" not looking away from Estelle's corpse Aerius smirked at the thought of taking his wife's life and proving to her God was real

"THEN FUCKING KILL ME ALREADY AND FREE ME FROM THIS HELL HOLE OF A LIFE AND MARRIAGE" Abigail threw her body with intense fiery that she jammed up the chains that bonded her feet breaking both her ankles from the tension that built up.

"It's not worth killing you" kissing Estelle's forehead Aerius walked back towards Abigail and closed the curtain. "You are the only living family I have, I've killed the rest" Abigail's eyes widen when she heard what Aerius said

"You killed our family?" Abigail questioned with a fumed tone she did not want to live any longer after hearing that

"You just think a gunslinger shows up at a Pastors house? I told him to hide their knowing that native couldn't tell them apart. Estelle was easy to kill she trusted me the most, that was a bad idea, and for Ambrose I just killed him today he was no longer a man of God and questioned everything I did"

"Did you pull Eliphaz's trigger too? Who else have you killed?"

"Knowing what I know about you I'm surprised you are still alive" shrinking against the wall Abigail was terrified.

"I never did anything to you…"

"Do you think me stupid Abigail?" Aerius shouted "I know who sent Eliphaz and my children down a dark path. It was you my dear!" Aerius snapped the cross from around his neck and threw his bible down "For what I'm about to do to you I don't want God to witness"

Chapter 6: Sword and Harkness

John stood hypnotized contemplating why did Natok call him by his last name he didn't remember a native helping with his killing. Walking away from Natok's blooding carcass John wanted to be as far from the lake as possible he didn't want to have to deal with more natives trying to kill him. "Waylon said he wasn't the only one how many people were needed to kill me?" John questioned out loud as he walked. "I need to find Aerius and kill him I just know he is behind all of this I want to see his heart in my hand as he is dying" noticing he was nowhere that he could recognize John looked ahead trying to peer through the heavy brush and high trees. "Where is that woman when you need her" remarked John thinking there was no hope for getting back to where he was. Just as he said that suddenly he was looking at clouds and the tops of trees it was as though he was flying but only using his eyes. "What is happening?" said John wanting to know how he could see from above and still have his feet on the ground. Hearing nothing but the cal of a single crow it soon settled with John that he was seeing through the crow's eyes and could find a way back to town. As the crow soared allowing John to see through its eyes it didn't take long for a line of smoke to be seen coming from a chimney stack. "I'll go there first" Said John as his normal vision came back to him.

Heading towards the smoking chimney John could hear voices nearby and gripped his knife. "Joseph, you going to church tonight, I heard Pastor Aerius was holding a special sermon tonight"

"I don't want to see that crazy old Christian Eli, You can tell he hasn't been the same since his daughter died" John hide behind a thick tree watching the two men. Joseph was thin with blonde hair that curled just touching his shoulders, he was dressed in torn clothing that made it obvious he had farmed fields his whole life. John noticed that

Joseph stood just slightly taller than the other man who was much older Eli's hair was slick black and wild just like the full beard that grew from his face he had a visible scar that took up the left side of his face stopping at his eye. "Come Eli you said you're Christian and wanted to go to church since you're back in town" Joseph nudge Eli in a joking manner trying to get him to smile but Eli's face did not change.

"I was a Christian this mark proves I am no longer welcome into heaven's gates" pointing to the scar on his face Eli glanced over at Joseph "You know how someone who believes in Christ gets a scar like this?" shaking his head no Joseph moved closer to see the scar in full detail.

"Looks like a gun wound, did someone shot you?"

"I did" tipping the pot they had boiling on an open fire Eli poured coffee into his mug "I needed to stop Satanic thoughts the devil was trying to use me as a puppet"

"So you shot yourself?" Joseph asked still looking at the scar lifting his hand to poke it only to have it slapped down by Eli

"Hah to get those devilish thoughts off my mind so I put a bullet in my head"

"Did they stop?"

"Of course however the hardest part had to be letting my family think I killed myself" Eli took another sip of coffee just as John came from behind the tree "Who are you?" he asked dropping his mug and drawing his gun

"My name is John I'm heading back to town and I couldn't help but over hear your conversation" sizing up both men John knew he'd have to shot one before they charged at him otherwise he couldn't take on both men at once.

"Harkness?" asked Joseph as his eyes widened he couldn't believe who he was looking at

"Excuse me Joseph was it, what did you call me?" untying the rope from his waist John used his strength to crack it like a whip having its breeze past Joseph's head.

"I called you Harkness, Waylon use to tell me stories about the town blacksmith when he was around that's what he called you" Joseph darted his eyes hoping the lie he was trying to spin could save his life.

"Whelp John my names Eli and I don't know who the hell you even are" Eli extended his hand to John who took it and shook it. "Why are you heading back to town?"

"I'm out for vengeance against those who killed my love and murdered me" drawing his gun Johns' target was Joseph but he held back from firing he was waiting to see if Joseph messed up and got catch up in his own lies

"John I hate to tell you you're not dead"

"No Eli he was dead I was at his hanging" continuing to listen to every word from Joseph's mouth John just wanted one mess up. "When someone is hanged a lot of the town's people always watch and in Harkne…John's case everyone who could come watch him die was there" remembering that he was cut down by Samuel what Joseph just said wasn't adding up if anyone who could be there was there then why didn't anyone stop Waylon from unloading eighteen bullets into his back or why didn't anyone stop the hanging. "We were told he murdered Pastor Aerius's daughter in cold blood so we were told to hang him"

"You killed Estelle?" Eli looked at John with such confusion as John begun to shake his head no "Joseph did you watch the hanging or did you help?"

"I watched it" retorted Joseph

"You say that but you also said we were told to hang him that's painting a different picture" John couldn't believe his eyes not only were Joseph's lie coming undone like he was waiting for but someone else had spotted it first and was calling him out on it.

"Yeah Joseph which was it?"

"I have to go see Pastor Aerius, Hopefully I'll see at church Eli" sprinting to his horse Joseph took off galloping into the trees

"He's hiding something from you John and I can sense it" Eli reached down grabbing his coffee mug off the ground brushing off the dirt "Made me drop my coffee coming from behind that tree"

"Hold that thought Eli I have a vermin to kill" running to the end of the trees John could hardly see Joseph on his horse he could only see a fading hind end. Drawing an arrow that he took from Natok's head John pulled back the bow sending a sharp arrow head right into the back of Joseph's leg pinching it to his horse.

"That's some aim you got their"

"First time I shot one of these things" throwing the bow onto the fire John glanced sideways at Eli "I'm not the only one whose suppose to be dead here"

"You remember me?" pulling his shirt down slightly showing a round scar under his collarbone John started laughing at Eli

"What blacksmith forgets the man who bludgeons him with the halt end of a sword, back from the dead?" remarked John he was intrigued on how Eli was standing in front of him.

"Had to leave after I shot the devil out of my mind although I'm starting to think I shouldn't have left" sitting on a close stump Eli peered into the fire breathing slowly "Everyone seems to hate Aerius since I left and Kathryn isn't anywhere to be found"

"It wasn't longer after you died that she killed herself in fact she used that sword you commissioned me to smith so you could purpose"

"Sad it really is but I was only with her because I couldn't be with the woman I lived"

"I'm on a mission of vengeance so either come along or stay here" John left Eli's side and walked start through the woods heading back towards town

"So you came back from the dead who helped you?" running to catch up with John who was a good distance in the woods Eli noticed that part of John's shirt was torn on the back and a branding of the cross could be seen.

"I came back for Vengeance I didn't kill my beloved Estelle"

"You sound like Orpheus but he went to the underworld for love you came back for it" stopping as he heard leafs crunch Eli drew his gun taking John instructing him to do the same. "Someone is here"

"I'm not afraid of anyone I can take them"

"From poison, to stabbing to hanging to shooting Harkness how the hell are you still alive after all that?" asked a shrouded figure standing between two trees

"Reveal your face!" shouted Eli who was standing between John and the shrouded figure

"My identity doesn't need to be known for me to kill Harkness"

"How many people want you dead?" Eli asked John who was standing with his gun in one hand and his knife in the other

"I don't remember so I have no clue how many were there"

"You should be died and I'll help you fix that" the figure ran towards Eli and John having a sword extended from the shroud, the same sword John forged for Eli.

"That blade belongs to Kathryn it must be returned to her" trying to protect John from the blade Eli stepped into the blades swing getting cut a crossed the back "You don't know what you are doing give me that blade"

"Eli stop blocking anything that is meant for me I can heal" jabbing his knife towards the figure John's blade caught the hood of the shroud cutting it straight down the middle revealing the figures face.

"Kathryn!" Shouted Eli has he dropped his gun running towards her "I was told you killed yourself with that blade"

"Move Eliphaz my fight isn't with you Harkness needs to die!"

"It's just Eli now and I won't let you hurt him" throwing his hands around the swords halt Eli attempted to pull it away from Kathryn.

"You really want to die for a murderer?" John picked up Eli's gun and pointed at both of them he didn't know what was going on anymore everyone he thought had killed themselves was still alive and it felt like everyone was out to try and kill him for something he didn't do

"I will shot you both if I have to" taking slow steps towards Kathryn and Eli who were still stuck in a game of tug-a-war over Kathryn's sword John placed the gun barrels into each person's forehead "Trigger is seconds from being pulled answer me"

"Shot me let me die" said Kathryn as she dropped her grip on her sword "You don't know how long I've been waiting" holding onto the sword Eli seen that his initials had been carved into it

"What's this?" asked Eli pointing to the initials on the sword

"That's love you idiot but you had to go shot yourself in the head" drifting her eyes from John to Eli who's eyes were still locked on the sword Kathryn could feel her heart fluttering, she hadn't felt that way since she first saw Eli in church when they were kids.

"I needed to rid myself of the devil's influence I'm sorry" Locking eyes Kathryn and Eli brought their hands together they had believed the other to be dead and now they had one another once again "I never stopped thinking about you Kathryn"

"I never stopped thinking about you Eliphaz… I'm sorry Eli" leaning in for a kiss Kathryn's body grew cold as she dropped to the ground with a bullet hole in her head

"WHAT DID YOU DO JOHN?" Eli shouted in shock

"She was here to kill me and I got to her first its life, now she really is dead"

"You can't just kill everyone you're acting like a demon" aiming the gun at Eli ready to pull the trigger John took a step back

"I am no demon" sending another bullet into Kathryn's body having seen her twitch John threw away his gun

"Not a demon but you do stuff like that" picking up Kathryn's sword holding it in front of John as a warning Eli walked backwards right up against a tree. "You're a vengeful person who's been reanimated from the dead that makes you a demon" knowing he had no way out of his own death Eli fall to his knees and spoke to the lord someone who he hadn't spoken with in years "Domine servus tuus sume me portas caeli" gearing up to send the sword through his stomach and kill himself Eli took one last look at Kathryn closed his eyes thrusting the sword towards his stomach

"That ain't happening!" remarked John as he ripped the sword for Eli's hand breaking the metal into twice pieces and throwing them into the woods. "You're going to help me find Aerius"

"Joseph said the Pastor was conducting a special sermon tonight"

"Good now who is he to you? You brought his name up" helping Eli to his feet John watched as a small silver cross came from under his shirt

"He's my older brother"

"Aerius is your older brother! I should have killed you when I had the chance!" placing his hands around Eli's throat attempting to choke him to death John was only able to hear subtle words

"He's gone…M….D"

"What speak up, I can't hear you" John remarked tightening his grip on Eli's throat

"He's…." Eli's eyes drifted into the back of his head as his windpipe was being crushed he could feel his breathing about to stop. Just as he was close to death John released his grip letting air back into Eli's lungs. "He's gone mad" taking deep breaths "that's what I was trying to say"

"I'm ready for mad you don't know what I've been through"

"We need to find Aerius he'll have all the answers to everything that's been going on"

"He is the answer to everything that's going on, I must kill him and Ambrose" bending down and grabbing the gun he dropped John knew he'd need it going against Ambrose again.

"Ambrose is still alive?"

"Only one of Aerius's three kids to still be alive but not for long" looking at John with confusion in his eyes Eli repeated what he heard

"Aerius's three kids?"

"Pastor got busy didn't you get the memo"

"I had to fake my own death remember how old are his kids"

"Ambrose was in late twenties, my beloved was eighteen when she was killed and Levi was sixteen when he was murdered by natives" John looked around trying to find a trail so he could exit the woods and go back to town.

"When was Levi born?"

"I didn't pay attention I just know Pastor's wife found out she was pregnant June of that year" finding the trail John followed it with Eli who stayed silent the whole time.

"We're back to town look their Joseph's horse" it was easy to see what horse belonged to Joseph since John had shot that arrow into his leg the horse had an arrowhead sized hole from where it went through Joseph's leg and got the horse.

"You foul vermin!" yelled John "You yellow belly parry dog" after the 2nd insult he threw out trying to bait Joseph out from whatever hole he was hiding in John had a tombstone catch his eye. The tombstone read *'Here lives John Harkness beloved Blacksmith and man of pure innocence'* why would someone curve him a tomb stone and who was kind enough to put that he was innocent on it.

"I'm coming for John" said Joseph his voice shaking

"You are going to die"

"Want a drink first friend nice way to get things off your chest?" As Joseph offered a despite drink to John it caused a flashback in his head. He remembered that same tone of voice and the same sentence from his last night alive he had went to the saloon for the first time and was told to go drink with the horse. Only one kind soul offered him a drink it wasn't until now that John was able to figure out the drink was poisoned and he could see Joseph's face in his memory.

"You really think I'll fall for that twice"

"It was worth a shot" shrugging his shoulder Joseph came out through the saloon doors. Giving John a glimpse inside the bar he hadn't seen since his fight with Waylon it was odd that nothing had changed. From what he could see the tables were still turned over and the Saloon Maiden was still drinking at the bar as the doors swung closed John watched as she mouthed something to him.

"Joseph you lied and ran, you should have a shot out with him" said Eli as he nodded his head to John

"Yeah a shot out sounds fun we should do that" moving towards each other until they could stand back to back Joseph and John waited for Eli to set the rules

"10 passes turn shot; the winner is still alive when it's done"

"Okay John you ready?" Joseph took a deep breath and lifted his foot to take his first step. "That's 1…2…3" as Joseph moved John stayed in the same spot he was listening to each number being thrown out "4…5…6…" just as Joseph went to count to 7 John turned around firing his gun missing by 1 inch "7…8…. What the hell Harkness"

"9…10" said Eli firing his gun right into Joseph's right eye which prompted John to fire too sending a bullet through Joseph's left eye blinding him

"Blind dog needs mercy and put down" pulling the trigger to his gun ready to take more vengeance John found out the gun was jammed and would not fire.

"Use this one" remarked Eli throwing John his gun

"Thanks Eli" taking Eli's gun John aimed it at Joseph ready to pull the trigger stopping to check the chamber "No bullets"

"I have them right here" handing John three bullets Eli used an intimidating face to keep Joseph completely still.

"You have ruined my life for the last time I walk this path alone" having the gun pointed John could feel Eli's breath that's how close they were together. Using the blunt end to bash Eli's face to disorient him John put down the gun using his bare hands to sever Joseph's head from his spine throwing it into the saloon.

"What did you do that for?" muttered Eli has he was holding his face

"You're becoming a threat and I don't like those" waiting for Eli to remove his hand from his eyes John aimed his gun at him firing sending a bullet into his heart.

"Tell Her I know now" waiting for him to shut up John stormed over and placed the gun onto Eli's esophagus unloading the last bullet.

"You are just like your brother pray to your God and see if you'll become that next Lazarus"

Chapter 7: Cult of Christ

"Aerius don't I'll be better" cried Abigail as she watched Aerius stomping towards her.

"Don't? Now you know that word! Where was that when you slept with Eliphaz?" reaching behind his wife Aerius pulled out a iron crafted bow staff and started swinging it at Abigail's leg adding more force with each swing "I don't want to hurt you"

"Then stop Aerius Stop for God"

"DON'T SAY HIS NAME! YOU HAVE NO RIGHT TO SAY THAT NAME!" Aerius swung the rod rapidly until he heard bone break "You wanted to break our marriage and destroy the vows we said before god I took your legs, after all you want to spread them for someone who isn't your husband"

"It was never meant to happen" Abigail bellowed having her whole body throbbing in pain she was ready to just die "Kill me Aerius this pain isn't worth living"

"You'd love that wouldn't you, I'm going to torment you until even God would not recognize your soul" going over to his work table Aerius pulled a steel safe from underneath "I've never gotten to use this and as a Christian man I had no reason" lifting a leather bond book covered in pentagrams from the safe Aerius could feel the power the book held. "You want to be my brother's whore I will cast your soul to hell and you can be Satan's"

"Either way I will be dead that's all I want I have no reason to live anymore" wanting to take action and show his wife true evil was soon replaced with the urge to just kill her and give her mercy

"I wanted you to feel the pain I carry and taste the evil that's been brewing inside me"

"I'm sorry Aerius" closing her eyes Abigail drifted off to sleep for the last time. Her injures were too much and she died.

"I was ready to give you mercy" flinging the book in his hand Aerius realized he hadn't been following Jesus the way the bible said to and he was living life picking and choosing. "What have I done I've killed them all! I am a murderer! How am I going to be welcome into the gates of heaven now?" Aerius cried scrambling to find his bible "I need to really know what you mean and not just carry you around" said Aerius to the cover of his bible. As he pulled himself together he found that he had remorse for what he did to John. That feeling didn't last long taking one look at the curtain that blocked Estelle's body for view sent him spiraling once again. "My dearest Abigail you may have died but even I know what you've wanted" placing his lip onto Abigail's looking past how cold they had become Aerius unchained her gently placing her on the floor. "I'm sorry about your legs do you forgive me?" when Abigail didn't answer Aerius punched her in the face which at this point was just a lifeless husk "You answer when your husband speaks to you!" he screamed shaking her body "Do you understand me?" Aerius placed his fingers over her mouth and made her lips look like they said yes even though her body was lifeless. As Aerius kissed down Abigail's body he became sickened with himself believing that he couldn't proceed without a blessing from God. "Heavenly father allow me this night, It has been so long for either of us and it would be approached" opening his eyes wide thinking the holy ghost touched his soul Aerius spend the night making love to the corpse of his dead wife forgetting all about the serum he was to preach.

When morning came Aerius gave one last kiss to Abigail before he left off for the church on his walk to the church he noticed town folks were all gathered around the foot of the church looking at something. "What's going on?"

"2 dead men lying on the steps of the church" replied a young man who was wearing an apron covered in flour he had ran from the bakery where he was needing dough for bread when he noticed it was time for church and rushed right over. "Good morning Pastor Aerius missed your sermon last night" said the young man as he saw Aerius approaching the church he had only seen Aerius because he had to divert his sight from the gruesome site.

"I dearly apologize I spent the night in with my wife. Why don't we go inside and I'll preach a serum so uplifting and full of blessings that even Jesus would say 'Amen'" noticing the young man didn't say anything Aerius took a closer look at the crowd and released they were all fixated on something. Seeing his congregation members standing shoulder to shoulder Aerius's curiosity took the better of him and he searched for a small view hoping he'd be able to see however he couldn't find any way to make the scene visible and gave up trying to see. "I must know what is going on outside my church this instant" Said Aerius with a firm tone

"There are two bodies outside the church" said the young man who addressed Aerius as he walked towards the church

"Everyone move" placing his palms together pointing them at the crowd Aerius gestured for everyone to move by opening his hands as though he was parting a sea

"One is Joseph and the other man... Well it's creepy Pastor he looks like you"

"Joseph was a good boy, who looks like me?" everyone stepped aside besides the young man in the floured apron he walked towards Aerius choosing to guide him to the bodies

"This man right here you are almost identical minus that scar" the young man pointed to Eli's body showing Aerius "Pastor does mean we won't be getting that amazing serum?"

"That's…that's…that's…"

"Are you okay Pastor you sound as though a ghost was amongst us"

"A Ghost is amongst us Simeon. That second body is my brother who was suppose to have died over nineteen years ago" walking over to Eli's body Aerius checked it for his silver cross removing it from his body.

"Should you be taking that off your dead brother Pastor won't he need it in heaven?" ask Simeon

"In Heaven you have no need for material things that tie you to the mortal world when you answer Heaven's call you are given everything you will ever need"

"So when we die our lord shows us how amazing life has been having him in our hearts by taking away our obsessive need for trinkets and material things?"

"Yes Simeon that is truly the blessing of our savior to one day be welcomed at his gates and feel his glories shine. He will be all we need"

"Amen" said Simeon capping his hands into a fist and pulling them to his chest "His is in my heart my soul is his to take"

"Take everyone inside the church my son and have them take a seat I will be in soon to preach" as Simeon guided everyone into the church Aerius knelt down in front of Eliphaz taking his hand draping the chain from his cross over his palm while he held the cross and begun to pray.

"I don't think you should be touching that Aerius" remarked John as he walked up right behind Aerius who was knelt down in front of Eli's body. "Come with me we need to have a word"

"I'm not going anywhere with you, I am mourning my brother's death and I have a serum to preach" without moving from his knelt potion Aerius signed for the church doors to be swung open wide.

"You're coming with me and I'll use force if needed. I hope force is need" cracking his knuckles right behind Aerius's head John was preparing himself for a fight, a fight he wanted but knew he most likely wouldn't get.

"I'm not going anywhere with you my people will take care of you for me"

"Only one you have left is Ambrose, I killed all the rest" hearing what John said made Aerius chuckle and his actions caused John to snatch him by the back of his neck "What's so funny?"

"John, I killed Ambrose and I always have people who will follow my every word" as Aerius lifted his hands to the sky the motion was seen by Simeon who was standing in the church doorway he alerted everyone and they turned to see what was going on outside. Once their eyes caught Aerius the whole congregation bowed their heads and begin to pray "Christianity is powerful and there are always new sheep to mindlessly flow the flock"

"You sound like a cult leader"

"Cult of Christ my son, just give your heart to the lord and you will be saved"

"I don't want to be saved, I am Vengeance!" John tightened his grip trying to crush Aerius spine but no matter how much pressure he put not even a bruise could be seen. It was as though John never touched Aerius with the intent to inflict pain.

"You see it's God's will for me to stay alive I am his conduit here on earth" pulling himself from John's grasp Aerius saw how much blood coated the front of John's clothing and looked back at the 2 dead bodies. "You killed my brother and a good kid for nothing"

"The kid wanted me dead in fact he poisoned me before" John looked at Joseph's body then at Eli's before facing Aerius "Your brother became a threat and you are next!"

"Am I really next? I think you'd prefer to know the men who hoisted the rope that hung you" gesturing his head left to a group of men who were all sitting in the first pew right up front inside the church "those men were working for me that night you were killed" falling into a blind rage John's sights changed from Aerius to the men he was just shown. Releasing his grip on Aerius's neck John stormed into the church he could only think about how he wanted to murder those men and what ways he wanted to do it

"You work for Aerius?" snarled John through clenched teeth

"Who wants to know?" replied a black haired man who had muscles large enough that they were ripping out of his shirt. The man took a look over to Aerius who slowly nodded which told him it was safe to talk to the enraged John. As John begun his altercation with the men who helped hang him Aerius walked into the church having Simeon help him barricade the door, he wanted to make sure John wasn't able to leave Aerius wanted to kill him dead and have him stay dead.

"I'm the man who you helped hang I saw your faces as I drew my last breath and now you will know the pain I suffered" the men couldn't take John seriously since he was still talking with his teeth clenched tightly they all started laughing which made John even more furious "I will peel the skin from your bones and feed the bones to your hounds" the more he allowed blinding rage to consume him the tighter his teeth clenched making his threats sound like someone trying to talk after being kicked in the mouth by a untamed mule.

"That man is dead you can't be him" said the black haired man trying to not encourage the notation to his friends.

"Sebastian that is John Harkness he has come back from the dead" said Pastor Aerius as he walked to his podium to retrieve the bible he kept in it. The pages hadn't aged well they had become yellow and needed to be handled with care, The passages had hand written notes from each pastor that had it before Aerius. His great grandfather willed that his ashes along with wood pulp from the red oak tree where his mother gave birth to him and where he gave his heart to the lord be used to make the pages, He believed by adding his own ashes that he would always be able to feel how much his family loved Christ and when they fault lost they could read from the pages and know he was there and would help them stay on the righteous path. Aerius's Grandfather had received the bible on the day he buried his father and on that day he felt his heart being pulled to Christ and he took up the mantel of Pastor helping many people open their hearts and convert. When he felt his mission was done he passed the bible to his son with instructions that when he passed pages would be added. He had written that his ashes were to be mixed with daffodil pollen forever solidifying that his eternal life was devoted to Christianity and that it was this mixture the new pages would be formed from. When Aerius had the bible placed in his hands when he turned sixteen he felt connect to his father that had long passed away due to smallpox. The bible had already had it's the spine replaced three times each time it was replaced more pages were added showing a more understanding view of the teachings of Jesus Christ. Aerius made a habit of reading the hand written notes that were etched in the margins he would even use them to draw inspiration for his sermons, it was in this bible he added satanic markings tainting it's rich connection to Christ making it a weapon for darkness even though he still used the handwritten wisdom from the pastors who came before him. It was this bible Aerius walked to get placing it on his podium opening it to a page he had drawn on using his own blood. The bible would have been to large if every page that came from previous pastors was put inside so there was a second bible created that housed all the pages pertaining to Satan and black magic. It was bound in leather and kept underground pastors feared the pages would taint anyone who was able to read it, They buried it inside a metal box and made sure to not explain to their descendants that it was created. Aerius discovered the metal box when he started digging out his hidden basement for the church it was this book that he kept by his work bench and attempted to use on Abigail before she died. He kept his family bible inside the church hidden away but added his own twist to it by craving in Satanic symbols.

"That man is dead Pastor we were there you paid us to hoist the rope" everyone in the church looked at Aerius when Sebastian said this, they weren't able to see the pages of the bible so they had just thought Aerius was beginning a serum and ignoring the visible fury burning in John's eyes however they all now looked at Aerius wondering if he was responsible for murder and if so was he some kind of devil that had been falsely leading them to believe in a God that may or may not be real.

"Ladies and Gentlemen of Christ this Man had done the most sinful thing a man could do and when I spoke with our lord he told me only death could vanquish the plague John Harkness brought to our town" failing to hone his congregation back from halting their trickling thoughts Aerius made on last attempt at trying to criminalize John "He walks amongst us and cannot be killed. I have seen him heal from the most fatal of wounds and he instills fear in those who do him wrong take Young Joseph's death it was this man who murdered that innocent soul, He even took the life of my brother who himself was a devoted follower of Christ just like all of you. Can you honestly sit here and turn your heart from your Savior Jesus Christ when there is concrete evidence we have an advocate of Lucifer himself amongst us at this very moment?"

"I feel our Lord in this room with me right now and he is saying that Pastor Aerius is correct and his actions were justified can I get an Amen?" preached Simeon as he shook his hands in the air to show he could feel Jesus was with him.

"Amen" spoke the congregation all in unison as they bowed their heads

"Are we just going to forget about me!" screamed John he couldn't take being ignored he wanted to kill someone and he wanted to kill someone now

"We didn't forget about you, We don't believe you to be John Harkness even if Pastor Aerius claims you are" Sebastian remarked raising from his seat "If you really were John Harkness you'd have a rope indent around your neck from the force my men and I used to hoist the rope" taking a gaze at John's neck Sebastian faced his men and gave a single nod to which all three men that were sitting with him rose up.

"Oh look it takes for you to see a dark bruise on black skin to see I am that man" John yanked on his shirt collar showing the rope markings that would not heal. "I am that man this is proof and I am back to get vengeance on those who killed my love" letting go of his shirt John squared up with Sebastian "The man you helped murder is Back!"

"You don't have to be" remarked Sebastian gesturing for his men to come by his side. "We can easily kill you again" chuckling which caused his belly to shake Sebastian couldn't help but think about how he enjoyed pulling that rope and he longed to do it again.

"It will be your funeral Sebastian and I'll slaughter your men too" huffed John as he head butted Sebastian. Stumbling back feeling his nose break Sebastian gazed over to Pastor Aerius who was lost looking into his bible.

"Pastor Aerius what do you want us to do with him?" out loud cried Sebastian as he set his nose by breaking it again giving himself two black eyes from the pressure.

"Bring him to him my son" Aerius pulled a vile from his pocket, the vile was completely silver and made to contain holy water only used for exercising demons, placing it next to his bible "Have each one of your men take a limb Sebastian and drag him here" clutching John by his right arm Sebastian started to drag him closer to Pastor Aerius. As he got closer to the podium John started to flail his limbs violently trying to punch Sebastian and break free of his grip that had started to leave bruises in the shape of fingers so visible that you could see every line and finger print from Sebastian's hand on John's arm. Instructing his men to assist him Sebastian found it was easier to force John into submission when four men had his limb and he had no chance of getting away.

"Here you go Pastor Aerius what should we do with him?" tightening their grip each time John thrashed the men felt warm blood trickling down their hands, they were holding so tightly that they broke the skin. "We've made him bleed so he can be killed" spoke Sebastian with a cheerful tone

"YOU CAN NOT KILL ME!" screeched John his voice echoing throughout the church

"When I say to everyone of you pull as hard as you can" said Pastor Aerius as he opened his vile placing his thumb slightly over the top. "I shell speak a prayer to the Arch Angel Michael asking him to exercise this demon from our lives once and for all.

"You might feel a slight pinch" said Sebastian jokingly to John who had stopped fighting and closed his eyes.

"Sancte Michael Archangele, defende nos in proelio. Contra nequitiam et insidias diabolic esto praesidium; Imperat illi Deus, supplices deprecamur; Tuque, Princeps militia caelestis, satanam et omnes spiritus malignos, qui per mundum ad perniciem animarum pervagantur,dei virtute detrude in infernum Amen" prayer Aerius as he sprinkled the holy water onto John's head

"Amen" said the four men each following the other

"Now destroy the vessel!" chanted Aerius loudly feeling his body filled with the Holy Spirit he could sense doing this exorcism was what God wanted him to do. Each man yanked John's limb in a different direction tugging as hard as they could until they were sent to the ground having their hands stuck deep inside John's flesh. They had ripped both his arms and leg completely off and were holding onto them. John's head and torso fell to the floor with a giant thud startling everyone in the church while the four men felt they had accomplished a great task sent from the heavens above. "The demon is gone and our lord is at peace Church is adjourn for today can I get an Amen"

"Amen" said the congregation in unison. Everyone piled out the front door leaving their bibles on the pews they didn't want to look at another dead body. They had forgotten that Joseph's and Eli's body still remained on the church steps and the patrons who left questioning their faith tripped over the bodies' landing right on top of them letting out a blood-curdling scream.

"I told you I wasn't someone to mess with John now you know" Looking down at John's body Aerius whole heartily believed he had killed him "You must of just been some Vengeful spirit who couldn't cut it" stepping from behind his podium Aerius pulled money from his pocket "I paid you before for helping murder him it is only fair I do the same this time" handing money to each man as he shock their hand Aerius felt relieved "You guys did a great job" thinking he had won Aerius leaned over the podium and pulled out the knife he used as a bookmarker in his bible. Locking eyes with the man who held John's left arm Aerius took it by the hand and started to cut severing John's hand off placing it in his bag. "Discard the pieces someplace safe. We will find a day to burn them and truly rid ourselves of John Harkness"

"Yes Pastor Aerius"

"That's a good boy Sebastian" remarked Aerius as he walked out of the church the bag he had John's hand in was dripping blood on the wooden floor "Don't forget to give a contribution to the church, All of you have committed a awful sin here today and it must be paid for"

"Sir?" said Sebastian with a questionable tone

"All four of you murdered a man and God has saw that, you must ask for his forgiveness and a contribution will do justice" placing his bag down Aerius turned to face Sebastian and the other men. "Murder is a sin Cain was punished and his heart blackened for his actions do you want that for you?"

"It just doesn't seem fair Pastor!" screamed one of the men as Sebastian stepped in front of him

"He didn't mean it sir. He's just a child"

"Move Bash it's about time someone stood up to this controlling asshole… Move or I'll move you Bash"

"Elijah don't we don't know what he's capable of doing" said another of the men as he stepped to stand next to Sebastian blocking Elijah from Pastor Aerius "We just participated in an exorcism in front of the whole congregation and they said nothing. I'm not sure how powerful Pastor Aerius's influence is"

"You too Josh great who isn't afraid of this bible driven asshole!" Elijah tried storming his way past Sebastian and Joshua only to fail and be pushed back by the two men.

"Let him past my sons he is allowed to have an opinion on what I say" reaching his hand out for Elijah to grab Aerius pulled him away from the men who held him back "Go ahead speak what you have to say"

"You paid us twice to kill the same man and NOW you claim it's a sin and we need to give a contribution! I heard you say that you killed Ambrose where's your contribution? Are you exempt from asking for Christ forgiveness? Or do you see our doing as the only unjust action that has taken place?" feeling as though he wasn't going to get an answer Elijah took a step closer standing only inches away from Aerius's face "I'm waiting for my answer do you only believe in Christ when his teaching and blessing benefit your life?" taking a deep breath Aerius only smiled at Elijah placing his hand on his shoulder

"My son I will answer every question you have but first I would like to know do you carry Christ in your heart?"

"Of course he is my savior and I follow my life in accordance to his teaches"

"Was one of his teachings 'Thou shalt commit murder for money'?"

"No, the fifth commandment is 'Thou shalt not kill' Pastor do not try to tie the bible into my actions" Sebastian and Joshua took a seat in a pew with the final man still standing he had yet to decide what his thoughts truly were on the subject.

"I can tie the bible into your life since you live by it my son" pushing his thumb into Elijah's shoulder Pastor Aerius leaned in close enough to whisper "If you even let out a sound I'll kill you"

"Get off of me!" Elijah said pushing Pastor Aerius "Hear I'm making a sound kill me you clearly don't want to answer my questions because I am right!"

"Children are never right you have not experienced who turmoil this cruel world has to offer. I have cradled you with my faith and this church as made for an internal spiritual crib. You will never know half of what life has put him through and for that I am sorry, just like Christ I love all my children equally and I am hard on you all for that very reason" Elijah moved from Aerius and walked over to the podium kicking it over

"I am not a child nor am I your child"

"Your actions proved to me you are just that look what you have done" seeing his bible laying on the wooden floor face up showing the page his satanic marking was on Aerius darted to close it helping no one saw.

"You are a controlling Monster everything needs to be your way otherwise its wrong. I've noticed that in your actions and how you preach and I know you have an obsession with that bible in particular and you claim that Jesus's teaches can be implicated into every decision we make. You say all that than have us assist in killing a man not once but twice THE SAME MAN AERIUS!"

"Elijah my son please claim down"

"Maybe Elijah is right" mumbled Joshua as he bowed his head

"What did you mumble Joshua?" Asked Aerius as his toned changed from compassionate to angry and resentful

"It was nothing"

"You could say it a minute ago when you mumbled but can't say it now" balling his hand into a fist Aerius swung at Joshua although just when he went to go back contact he open his fist and used his bare palm to smack Joshua leaving a bright red hand print that stung

"It was nothing" whined Joshua bowing his head down as low as he could not wanting to look at Aerius or show that he was holding his face hoping the pain will go away.

"No one you have any respect for me and I my own Church you think just because you are adult that you have it all figured out. Well you don't life is going to get harder and you'll ever be broken by it or you'll grow from it" Aerius moved over so that he was by all four men "Look at me all of you" demanded Aerius clapping his hands together to get their attention "Now I don't have all day to deal with this" All four men looked at Aerius fear coating their eyes "I have so much I could teach you about life and I have so many experiences that bring wisdom and knowledge, You just have to be open to learning these things. I won't force anything on you I am not your father but I hope you see me with enough to respect that I am like a father figure in your eyes. Yes you did a bad thing and giving a contribution to the church would have been a great way to repent what you failed to realize because you think you have anything all figured out is that I never said it had to be money. I just said to pay a contribution" Stopping to gaze at the four men Pastor Aerius started to think would he have had these conversations with Ambrose if he hadn't of killed him or would he of had it with Levi if he didn't orchestrate him murder "As for you Elijah someday you have the fine makings of a honest and truth worthy follow our Christ however you need to get over having an issue with Authority and learn to deal with the consequences from your actions and tone of voice."

"I don't have an issue with Authority I just believe that everyone needs to be heard and rightfully heard"

"There you go with that demanding tone again Life isn't fair you need to learn that and I'm sad to say it but someday when I'm not here to protect you that attitude of yours will get you killed. On the contrary with how you've been acting not just in church today but during your everyday life thinking the church and myself can just bail you out your actions might end up getting me killed because Ole Pastor Aerius will have to fix the issue"

"You don't have to apologize for my actions I'm not your child so stop acting like my father"

"I am everyone's father! I am Christ voice on this earth and we are all his children"

"Pastor why haven't you really answered Elijah's questions you're just laying into all of us especially him for speaking his mind. I would like to answer your answers please sir" the four man who was unsure how he wanted to react in the situation had finally spoke and he wanted to know more details not just what he was seeing with his eyes, he wanted to know what Aerius had going on in his mind and why he was dodging everything.

"Yes of course I will answer the questions Zachariah thank you for being so polite and waiting until I'm in the middle of giving an amazing talk that will help shape your future" hearing the sarcastic tone that followed Aerius's words Zachariah knew what was about to come but stood his ground waiting. "I am not exempt from asking Christ for forgiveness. I have always prayed for forgiveness in this very church. When I do have to give a contribution I throw a penny down the well behind the church and I sit and read the bible out loud"

"You have two more Pastor Answer them please"

"NO your acts today weren't the only unjust I would say mine were as well. I could of closed the church down to perform the exorcism but instead I locked the whole congregation inside to bear witness" turning to face the door Aerius stopped swinging around and punching Zachariah in his mouth causing him to spit up blood " Don't you dare think you can just stay silent the whole time than get demanding. Please Pastor Please Pastor you must be the strong silent one who calculates decisions before he makes them where was that logical thinking when you helped murder the same man twice!"

"That logical thinking was processing the fact you only believe in Christ and his teaching when it benefits your life. That's fine Aerius but at least admit it and for a Christian pastor what's with the satanic markings inside that bible? I know you only carry it around to showcase you have faith but you've lost your sight on its true teachings and for that you have damned your soul"

"Zachariah that's what you truly think of me?" Aerius asked with a devastated look

"Many people in this town think that of your but you are so controlling that no one wants to stand up to you. Elijah was right when he said you are a monster, He was even right when he used the term asshole. You don't know when to leave anyone alone and you don't to be involved in everything no wonder Estelle never told you she loved John. You would have just ruined that. OH wait you did Aerius" picking up the podium that Elijah kicked over in a fit of rage Zachariah stood behind it "It's your turn to here a serum and if you don't like it to damn bad sit your ass down" patting the pew so that Aerius would sit next to him, Sebastian who had remained quit during all the arguing was ready to leave the church and hide what was left of John body but he knew that whatever Zachariah was going to say could be impactful since he doesn't always speak. "You have planned all this so the blood is on your hands Aerius! You killed Ambrose his blood is on your hands! You had us kill John once for loving Estelle and again for coming back because he loved her that blood is on your hands! You threw a fit when she had to go to the smithy alone when the church was in need of John's serves You clearly could have went instead of her!" slamming his fist on top of the podium as he saw Aerius attempt to get up Zachariah wanted to make his presence known "You were so afraid of your birth children grow up and living a life that wasn't how you deemed fit that you much rather them be miserable or dead! Estelle was over the moon for John she loved every second they could sneak away and be alone together. They'd talk about life, joke and even sneak a passionate kiss of two that all stopped though when John noticed you picked what parts of him you respect. You never even gave him a chance to prove he could have been the best for Estelle, Aerius you didn't even know about their relationship! You were the only one who didn't!" jumping up infuriated Aerius was livid after hearing the way Zachariah was talking to him

"I didn't want them together because he was a Negro, Estelle needed a respectable white man to marry and start a family with! I will not sit here and be belittled like some insolent child.

"Yes you will Pastor" placing his hands on Aerius's shoulder Elijah forced him back down into his spot next to Sebastian.

"Skin color is a hang up for you? Mr. Satanic symbols in a Christian bible glad we know where you draw the line. I already see those wheels turning you're wondering why she fault so comfortable telling me and not just coming to you with it. That's simple even if you had been okay with her dating John you would have just assumed that all he wanted was sex and that's it. When in reality he was so in love with her the only thing he cared about was making her happy and he even tried to make you happy by giving the church all the supplies needed. Yes Aerius this very church we are standing in was built with all free materials that would have cost the church quite a bit all because the Blacksmith was in love with your daughter. He gave you so much and each time you said this would be better or we should fix this next without even a thank you although you claimed to be grateful and kept saying you'd pray for him"

"Seems like someone isn't as much of a saint as they think they are" commented Sebastian as he smirked away

"Tell me Zachariah, She felt so comfortable talking to you why?" asked Aerius trying to focus the conversation on one part and distract everyone from what else had been said. He was attempting to manipulate the room back in his favor and have control of the conversation.

"Do you remember a woman named Rebekah Strauss?" questioned Zachariah

"No I don't remember a woman named Rebekah Strauss" rolling his eyes Aerius didn't want to answer the question he didn't want to think about the one sin he commit against his wife that almost cost him his marriage. He didn't want to remember the slim tiny German girl who caught his eye one summer day while the heat was blistering down. He had traveled by horseback to preach the word of God a few towns over justifying it to his wife by saying that the immigrants that just settled that land didn't know the blessed word of Christ and as a preacher it was his duty to show everyone how much joy Christ can bring into your life if you open your heart. As he stood above everyone preaching not many were able to understand him most didn't speak fluent English. When he was done he walked to everyone taking their hands into his praying for them, it wasn't until he got to a young woman dressed in a patchwork dress made of black and grey patches, The young lady held her head down when Aerius walked up to her all he could see was the red pompom on top of her bollenhut hat he was able to see her face while he preached but why did she have it down now. As he gracefully cupped her hands in his the young woman lifted her head smiling her eyes pierced Aerius's and he knew in that moment that she understood everything he had preached. Once he started his prayer for her she started to repeat his every word keeping deep eye contact with him the whole time. Once the prayer was done and Aerius could get a better look at the young woman he was smitten her figure was slimmer than his wife Abigail and he felt warmth from her smile, he only felt regret and disappointment when Abigail looked at him. He even noticed the young woman was tiny she only came up to his chest when they were next to each other and that he liked believing a woman his height had to be seen as an equal but someone shorter could be broken mentally until they did everything he said without question. The last thing he noticed was that the young woman had charcoal black hair with a single streak of red down the side. Aerius couldn't help himself he wanted this young woman but how would that look if a Pastor slept with someone in his new congregation. He made the decision that he would convince this woman to sleep with him and when he was done he would say that the town all shun the Blessing of Christ and no one should go there. It didn't take much and that very night Aerius convinced the young lady to come to his room that's when she told him her name was Rebekah Strauss and she revealed just how much she loved him by removing her dress and giving herself to him. When they woke Aerius asked if she would translate his sermons that way the others would understand and from that day until he had to leave everything Aerius preached was translated by his new lover Rebekah. On his last day Aerius knew he couldn't take Rebekah back home with him but he didn't want her traveling to look for him so he had to break her heart saying that he never loved her and that he had to get back to his wife, hearing the man she loved already had a wife Rebekah slapped Aerius repeatedly on his chest being overwhelmed with emotions. It was this woman Aerius didn't want to remember he thought that dark part of his life of buried.

"I figured you'd say you didn't Father! That's right Aerius all these years I've been coming to your church and watching your every move idealizing you as a Pastor it's because you are my father"

"I only have 1 son and he is dead!" hearing what just slipped out of his mouth Aerius dashed for the door grabbing his bag that contained John's hand and ran off.

"He couldn't handle the truth" said Zachariah as he came from around the podium and started picking up John's limbs "We need to hide these until we are able to burn them that Aerius was right about" traveling to the Sawmill Sebastian, Elijah, Joshua and Zachariah felt it would be the perfect place to stash John's limbs since the Sawmill was owned by the church and only those closet to Pastor Aerius knew the correct was to enter.

Chapter 8: Bone

Having his body feel like melting play dough John felt his limbs snarl crawling towards each other trying to reform. "Aerius has my hand that asshole" as John felt his legs pull back together he decided that from here forth he wasn't going to hold back no more remorse for people he was just going to hurt them all "I need to find them all every time I think I've killed them I discover more people at fault" dragging his foot behind him as he refused John could hear an electric saw whining and ran full sprint to see where the sound was coming from as he approached the sound he could see a sawmill worker was cutting wood. "I wonder if this'll hurt" John thought to himself as grabbed the worker and pressed his face down on the saw sending bits of flesh and blood into the machine causing it to bind and smoke, the workers face was still stuck to the saw twisted into the blade. "I WANT AERIUS!" blurted out John as he ripped the worker from the machine seeing how mangled his face had gotten.

"You can't be here leave before things get worse for you" yelled the foreman when he noticed John standing by the running saw with one of dead workers in his hand

"Bring him to me!"

"Who do I need to bring to you?" retorted the foreman as he ran towards John cooking his gun

"I want Aerius! Bring him to me!"

"You want the Pastor? Haven't seen him in weeks but some friends of his frequent here a lot"

"Take me to them now!" screamed John snatching the gun from the foreman bludgeoning him with the handle "Take me to them now! I won't say it again!" spinning the gun in his hand John pulled the trigger shooting the foreman straight through his stomach "Screw this I'll do it on my own" cocking the gun back one more time John fired blowing off the foreman's head "Everyone is going to die by my hand until I have Aerius!" moving through the sawmill John spotted Sebastian and swung the gun he was holding like a bat aiming for his head.

"You still pissed from Aerius? You don't need to try and hurt me Elijah"

"Do I look like Elijah?" John said aggressively

"How is this possible? How are you alive?"

"It's called Vengeance!" echoed John his voice sounding a little distorted from all the abuse to his neck and body "I want Aerius! Bring him to me!"

"I won't be bringing you anyone do you want to be ripped in half again" remarked Sebastian signing for Zachariah, Joshua and Elijah who were nearby

"I don't plan on it this time you'll meet your fate"

"You want to act touch but deep down you're afraid of what we might do to you" John stepped to Sebastian pressing his face to his

"I'm ready when you are"

"Guys lets teach this child a lesson" As Elijah approached John he fired off the gun he had instantly killing Elijah, he threw a punch knocking Zachariah away and then he got jumped and hold by Joshua and Sebastian.

"Bring it on" struggling to break free John jabbed his finger into Joshua's eyes blinding him for the rest of the fight "I told you this time was going to be different" John backed up and ran towards Sebastian leaping towards him turning his body into a sprawl tunneling through Sebastian leaving nothing but a hollow whole right where his chest should be Sebastian fell dead landing on Elijah who had already been killed by John.

"You two are next!" John turned his sights to Joshua and grabbed the closet weapon he could swinging the two by four as though he was playing golf connecting the end of the wood to Joshua's glass chin shattering it on contact. "One more for good measure" stepping over Joshua so that his head was between his feet John aimed the wood downward smashing Joshua's face pushing his brains out the sides of his head. "Don't think I forget about you" sliding the bloody two by four along the ground John chucked it at Zachariah falling short by a foot.

"I can take you to Aerius Just don't kill me" pleaded Zachariah holding his hands up in defense with his palms out hoping for mercy.

"You don't know where to find Aerius, you lie"

"I've watched him in secret for years I know where he hides away and I can take you as long as you don't kill me" thinking over his options John contemplated if he was being told the truth or if it was a ploy so he'd let his guide down "He has a cellar under the church I was there when it was dug out, He claimed it was for church storage but we keep having to move the pews back and forth so he must use it for something else" noticing the look in Zachariah's eyes John decided to trust him on this one things. He remembered helping Ambrose move the pews and collect bibles so it wasn't too hard to believe that others had to move them as well.

"Take me to Aerius and I won't kill you"

"You don't know how much this means I am so grateful" shaking John's hand vigorously Zachariah couldn't hold back his joy all he had to do was take John to Aerius who was most likely hiding away in the churches cellar.

"You don't deliver and I'm ripping that Adams' apple out with a pair of tweezers then boiling you over a hot spring until your flesh is malleable and your bones are soft" swallowing his joy Zachariah gestured for John to follow him. "What do I call you?"

"Everyone has always called me Zachariah"

"Zach it is!"

"Please don't shorten my name"

"You want me to say Zachariah every time I address you" left bewildered John couldn't see why anyone wanted to go by their full name when a shortened version that was simpler for everyone to say existed. "Why is it that important to you Zach…Zachariah" scuffing at the thought of having to say that name every time he addressed him pissed John off

"My Mother always told him that my Father wanted my name to be Zachariah and until recently I had never met him figured if I went by Zach he wouldn't recognize me"

"That is the dumbest load of horse shit I've heard, did he recognize you when you met him?'

"No, He even denied ever knowing my mother which made me angry"

"Claim down little ball of disappointment I'm not here to therapist you through your daddy issues. I just want to kill the man who took everything from me" Zachariah stopped and just started breathing his eyes fixated on a trickling leaf that was making its way down to the ground from the highest tree top. "Fuck you stop for?!"

"Who killed Estelle?" asked Zachariah slowly breathing "Tell me John I can handle it I watched Levi get scalped and I know Aerius killed Ambrose, So Please tell me who Killed Estelle?"

"Ambrose Killed Estelle"

"What! That can't be! He wouldn't have done that to her WHY?" shouted Zachariah as he stood in place with his arms clenched by his chest shaking his fist in the air

"Aerius told him to and he followed his orders"

"Bet disobedience is what got him killed Aerius threatened to kill Elijah after we ripped you apart"

"Interesting why would he do that?"

"Elijah was standing up to him and you know Aerius everything needs to be his way otherwise he blows his top" stroking his chain feeling how death like his flesh was becoming John sensed he was running out of time

"You need to get me to Aerius faster!"

"I can only take you as fast as our feet can go I'm Sorry John"

"Who puts the Sawmill on the county line when the main part of town has everything, what idiot thinks of something like that!" kicking the dirt John felt he had lost and would never get vengeance on Estelle's killer. All he had to do was find out who really killed her and made Ambrose take the fall but *"WHO?"* he thought *"Who would want someone so sweet and innocent dead?"* as he thought to himself he went over a list of suspects that had something against Estelle but he kept coming up empty everyone in town loved her. He loved her most of all though and that's what got him killed, *"If Aerius could have poisoned, hung and shot me himself he would have. He hated me with a fierily fury that burned almost as hot as his love for his lord"* putting together list of people who wanted him dead was a lot easier he only had one friend who didn't want him dead and Estelle herself, Everyone else was either using him or they wanted him dead.

"We're almost there just little ways to go" hearing Zachariah's voice broke John from his inner thoughts and he wasn't too happy, they weren't fully about Estelle but she was there and even if it was just in his thoughts at this point he would take it.

"Good I was starting to think you lied and were going to try to attack me"

"If I wanted to do that I would have thrown saw dust in your eyes and used the lumber hoist to impale your chest leaving you suspended in mid air until you expire"

"What makes you think I expire?"

"We tore you apart and you reformed I don't think your body could handle much more impacts like that" John stopped he didn't know what to say Zachariah had noticed what was going on with him was that his plan watch as John slowly started to become nothing but bones to destroy him. What was going through his head?

"You seem to know more than you've lead the others to believe" suspiciously asked John

"I watch what is going on around me and make my decision based on that" Zachariah stopping walking his eyes fixated on the church seeing Aerius standing at the top of the steps. "We are here and there he is" nodding his head towards the church Zachariah noticed a small crow fly above them over head.

"This is where my vengeance becomes my glory" charging towards the church with pain in his heart for the lost of his beloved Estelle was not the best decision John had made. When he was a mere sprint away Aerius pulled a rifle from behind his back and shot John in the forehead sending him to his knees.

"I know that won't kill you boy but this part is going to be my favorite" stepping down from the churches steps Aerius grabbed a gardening hoe that was leaning on the wall and swung it driving it inside the side of John's face shattering his jaw and severing his skin deep enough it cut through muscle. "That should do it. A few more heavy blows will kill him for good it's that what you theorized?"

"Yes Father" Zachariah walked to Aerius who had his hand gestured out

"So he should be dead?"

"Yes Father" kicking John's body Zachariah noticed slight movement but kept his mouth shut

"Let's celebrate by doing this" pointing the rifle he was still holding at John's head Aerius unloaded the chamber smiling as he fired the remaining rounds "It feels great to have finally killed him ashamed what I had to do the first time"

"The first time John was killed?"

"Yeah for people to see what kind of demon that coon really was I had to sacrifice my own child"

"And by sacrificed you mean?" Zachariah asked bewildered on what that could mean

"Meaning I had to kill her"

"Her?"

"Yes my daughter, your half-sister" grabbing Zachariah shaking him Aerius watched as his face turned white than to red than back white again

"John said Ambrose killed Estelle on your orders"

"I had already killed her before I sent Ambrose her body didn't even have time to cool it was still warm"

"YOU KILLED ESTELLE?" Screamed Zachariah

"You would have done the same when you discovered she was in love with the town's shadow, He's a villain and he was a demon sent back from hell to destroy us all"

"Villain, Demon, town shadow! You don't hate him because he wasn't a good fit for her. You hate him because he's black. ARE YOU FUCKING KIDDING ME?" Zachariah yanked the gardening hoe out from john's face "from what she told me he was a good man"

"She was blinded!" said Aerius quickly wanting nothing to do with a conversation that involved Estelle's relationship with John

"She loved him Father you were the blind one and could not see that"

"Don't lecture me about my feeling towards something I loathe" Aerius looked down seeing every bullet hole inside John had begun to heal and his body was twitching "You said John was dead and could stay dead"

"Did I?"

"Yes you did!" Aerius yelled flailing his arms in the arm

"Must suck being told a lie from someone who you thought cared about you. My mother felt that way when you left her to go be with Abigail and your other kids after saying you'd never leave"

"I have no time to discuss your whore of a mother NOW do as you are told boy" the crow that Zachariah saw had landed on top a close tombstone and just watched him. "Grab the sledge if his soul doesn't want to cross over and met our lord then I'll torture him in the same manner"

"You can't crucify him, He's already dead"

"Flesh is flesh he will still know" feeling as Aerius placed a rail spike on his wrist John leaped up and turned towards the crow that just cawed at him "WHY WON'T YOU DIE!" Aerius screamed stomping his right foot on the ground. The setting sun encapsulated John in its flittering rays using his shadow to cast the silhouette a crow over the front of the church.

"Vengeance does not rest Aerius" passionately said John in a blind anger

"Dear lord what will it take to rid this demon from your divine world?" prayed Aerius falling to his knees at the front of the church he had finally hit his breaking point and was done with John.

"Pray to your God, He won't save you"

"My lord is righteous he will save me from you"

"Just like he saved those innocent lives you took" John stormed up to Aerius grabbing the bag that held his hand in it. "This is mine!" holding his hand up to the nub he had John waited for the two limbs to reform together which only took a few minutes.

"You are sick Harkness" confidently said Simeon with a slight hint of confusion when he used John's last name only.

"I see your lap dog has returned to give you, for lack of better phrase, a hand"

"That's right I have!" said Simeon trying to hold off the crackles in his voice. "I'm here to help kill you"

"How many times do you people have to be shown I cannot be killed?" John said as he grabbed at Simeon's throat "I'll rip it out everyone back up"

"Do it Harkness I have followed my Lord and will be welcomed by him" looking at Zachariah who was standing quite trying not to look at John

"Another Religious foul who is willing to die in such a rush, There's no one to met there I should know"

"Religion is a man-made term to try and overshadow the Presence of our lord. The world wants you to have free will when it comes to what you believe in because men are afraid of the truth" mumbled Simeon as John gripped his throat tighter with every word

"You sound just like Aerius when it comes to that smoke and mirrors magic man scam, Zach help me out here" throwing Simeon down directly at Zachariah's feet John watched as the man backed up using his eyes to roam the room, stopping when he saw Aerius as to ask for permission to act. "You begged me for your life in that Sawmill now you can't even asset in helping me kill! What is wrong with you?"

"I just don't like killing people I'd rather keep blood off my hands that's all"

"You want to keep Blood off your hands! ARE YOU SERIOUS?" John pulled the blade he carried from his waist line and threw it at Zachariah's head who watched it wiz by stabbing into the wall right next to his eye. "Let me do something I don't do, I'll repeat myself just so we are clear and to prove I heard you correctly" kicking Simeon in his stomach when he walked up to Zachariah to retrieve his knife from the wall John lend forwarded so he could look Zachariah directly in his eyes " You…want…to…keep…blood…off…your…hands! There I even said it slow so you could really comprehend what you just said to me"

"I know what I said John you don't have to be an asshole about it"

"Don't have to be an asshole? You must be the most idiotic person I have ever met! Do you spend a lot of time with Aerius?" as the name left his mouth John got a painful reminder that Aerius was still in the room.

"Silver candle holder the weight should bring back memories you crafted it for the church" bashing the candle holder across John's back Aerius saw blood had got onto it "you've gotten blood on it that's such a shame" Aerius took the candle holder swinging the base end at John's temple bashing his skin open "Oh No I got more blood on it what should I do?" sarcastically muttered Aerius who was ready to swing again when he noticed Simeon laying on the ground wheezing for air "Simeon get up and get yourself together"

"Yes Pastor Aerius" Simeon said as he struggled to get off the floor having to reach an arm out to Zachariah to help him fully to his feet. He was having issues breathing and the stomach of his shirt was soaked in blood. When John kicked him it didn't just hurt enough to leave a bruise it was impactful enough to burst his skin open and cause internal bleeding which was all seeping out onto his shirt. "I've changed my mind I'm not ready to die, Help me sir"

"You will not die. Help me first than we shell pray to Christ and he will hear your pile. He's merciful and has healed the injured many a times; you can be his miracle of triumph"

"My heart is open to his eminence He is the truth in this world of lies and fairy tale beliefs. He is the only one and everyone will know how amazing he is once they open their hearts like I have" Simeon took two steps towards Aerius and fell down on one knee "Pastor Aerius could we do that prayer right now, I'm not feeling my best, I don't want to die sir" cried Simeon his eyes filling with tears "SAVE ME LORD, YOU ARE MY SHEPERHERD, I AM NOT READY TO JOIN YOUR PRESENCE IN THE GLORY THAT IS HEAVEN, PLEASE LORD I AM BUT A HUMBLE SERVANT OF YOUR DEVINE TEACHINGS, PLEASE SAVE ME!" said Simeon as the tears he was crying poured down his face

"That is a man of God you should take lessons Zachariah"

"Yes Pastor Aerius" holding his head down not looking up from his shoes Zachariah could sense he would have to pick a side between John and Aerius, *"should I tell John the truth or should I side with Aerius he is my father, I have to honor my father. What's the right thing to do?"* thought Zachariah to himself even as Aerius was address him

"I'm in tears myself seeing how powerful Christ is in that boy's life. Not much chokes my up but I am so blessed to be able to believe in such an amazing man, Jesus Christ is wonderful and I hope you learn that one day my son"

"Someone kill whiney So we can go back to wanting each other dead" remarked John grabbing the back in Simeon's hair pulling his head back until it was tilted "I have a knife I can do it or do one of you want to give him mercy?" John waved his knife at both Zachariah and Aerius who didn't care to face him "I'll do it!" placing his knife against

Simeon's throat slowly adding pressure so that I'd break the skin John stopped blurting out in laugher

"What's so funny?" questioned Simeon who was shaking afraid of the knife that was pressed to his neck

"You seem to be more intoned with your faith than Aerius and he's a Pastor, You must read the bible and obey its teachings?" pulling the blade from Simeon's neck John helped him to his feet "my fight is not with you, You were brought in to this as a pawn, I want the king who isn't afraid to sacrifice his own men to cover his ass"

"My life is the bible the lord's teachings are in my every step. I was told to call you Harkness and fight you until I could kill you"

"You are blowing everything gaining that conscience, Take this and hurt him now" taking the bloody candle holder and wrapping Simeon's hand around it Aerius was not pleased. "Use this and hurt him!"

"This is not God's way Sir"

"You think you know God's way? God's way is to slowly kill you!"

"He will heal me when we pray" said Simeon bowing his head as he kneeled down on one knee crossing an arm over his chest "I am his solider here on earth"

"Pawn" coughed John

"You are such a waste of a follower; you can't complete a simple task even in the name of the lord. We are casting out the demon John Harkness has become" pushing Simeon out his way Aerius took another swing with the candle holder again hitting John in his temple again

"Zach you going back to being silent or are you afraid?" asked John hoping to get as answer

"I've picked a side" Zachariah responded as he turned to face John holding the second candle holder "You are right I do have blood on my hands"

"About time you use that brain of yours" walking over to a crying Simeon lifting him to his knees "I'm here to help relieve your pain"

"Are you going to help me pray?" cried Simeon

"Even better our lord would want this" Zachariah shoved the candle holder down Simeon's esophagus banging it down with his bare fist. "There you can rest now" standing in front of Aerius and John taking steady deep breathes Zachariah knew whose side he needed to pick "Someone had to bring him mercy I was that guy. My name is Zachariah, not Zach. I don't want to go over it a third time with you do you understand?"

"Yeah I understand after that I know you weren't bluffing about what you could have done in the Sawmill" John smiled at Aerius "your man is on my side, so tell me Aerius who killed Estelle!"

"I KILLED MY DAUGHTER ESTELLE!" screamed Aerius as he realized everyone seemed to find away to bring up his actions and what he could now see was wrong. "Is that what you wanted to hear that I am the one who killed Estelle?" John froze wondering how he didn't see it sooner. He had gone over the list of people who wanted him dead and what tactics Aerius used to pull off such a feat.

"You should run!" John said looking at Zachariah who had moved closer to Pastor Aerius

"When I first heard my sister was dead I was in shock just how John is right now" Zachariah stretched his arm behind his back and pulled a sharpened butchers blade from underneath his shirt "I already knew how happy she was with John, She wrote so much in our letters about him and this town". "Today I feel no remorse you have me numb father but he must be taken care of first" Zachariah and Aerius looked at John as they both grabbed weapons whaling blows onto John "Father Get your gun these objects have become blunt and battered"

"My son we have something no one else has even thought about using" dragging a giant crate out from behind the wall John could see what Zachariah had done.

"Aerius you call everyone son but that tone is what you used on Ambrose when he acted up at church"

"You went to church?" Zachariah questioned he had never seen John come into the church and if he did walk in the door hinges squalled letting out an alarming sound that everyone could hear distracting them from the Pastor who was preaching the word of God.

"I waited outside up against the wall adjacent to the door, I could hear everything and I would even find myself reading the bible when times got tough. That was something I was doing for Estelle. She wanted me to go to church and find Christ. She didn't find him inside some church she found him out in the open but hoped it'd be different for me if I saw it firsthand"

"Stop talking about her like she is dead!" Aerius said becoming filled with shame and regret over saying what he did

"She is dead!" John said

"Jesus will bring her back like he did Lazarus with enough prayer" Aerius groaned

"She can't come back from the dead, I am only here for vengeance against you" scuffed John throwing a punch at Aerius

"Jesus can bring her back and I can prove it!" Aerius smiled showing all his teeth keeping eye contact with John

"You better not be lying to me Aerius, If you are so help me I'll mangle your face so bad your God wouldn't recognize you" jabbing Zachariah in the throat casing him to struggle to breathe John felt happy "That's for turning on me once you seen Pastor Aerius"

"I…Didn…'t…ha…ve…a…chose" said Zachariah through breathless lungs as he struggled to get the full word out.

"He's the reason he begged for your life?" a shocked John sat down trying to wrap his head around what was unfolding around him

"Yes, Pastor Aerius is my father; I am on his side when it comes to standing up to you. The bible says I must be"

"After all this I need a drink" feeling his body go into a trance as he sat on the church pew John closed his eyes. When he opened them the color was completely gone not even a trace where an iris and pupil would be visible, they were like two long brightly lit corridors that dropped off into an even brighter abyss if you could ever find the end.

    As John did this he was using his connection to the crow to see through its eyes and guide it to the saloon hoping it would be corporative and beneficial in gathering him a bottle to drink. He was ready to drink himself to death, if that was even possible, for having to deal with Aerius and Zachariah's newly discovered daddy issues. Soaring through the space above the saloon door John could see the place had finally been straighten up no more broken glass or destroyed furniture like; tables, chairs, walls and bar tops all over the place it looked nice. "Take your ass out of my saloon" said the Saloon

Maiden swatting a broom at the crow causing it to caw and fly straight up dodging the brush end of the broom "I don't have time for your shit today" she said trying to hit the bird again. While John was seeing through the crow's eyes dodging a weaponized broom Aerius and Zachariah were standing over his body.

"What do you think is happening to him?" asked Zachariah

"Hopefully this is him dying"

"You hate him for being black but not me for being a bastard yet it is I who the bible condemns to hell just for being born" Zachariah gazed at Aerius with regret in his eyes and sorrow in his soul remembering how Aerius acted when he brought up his mother.

"That's just it Zachariah you weren't meant to be a bastard, I had planned to divorce Abigail and marry your mother just before you were born that is why you have such a pristine name" meeting the gaze Zachariah was giving him Aerius felt the ends of his mouth start to form a smile that he struggled to fight off. "I didn't divorce Abigail because she ended up pregnant with Levi whom up until recently I thought was my son. Turned out he was the only child of my brother Eliphaz who faked his own death just to come back into town and murdered by John Harkness"

"Our lives seem to be plagued by that man"

"First he claims your sister's heart and brain washes her so bad she gives him her chastity before wedlock resulting in her being pregnant than he gets killed just to come back and murder the remainder of our family"

"John only killed Eliphaz who at that point went by Eli. Father you killed the others, it was you who murdered Estelle and you who killed

Ambrose. You came clean you told me yourself, Why blame John for that?"

"He is to blame for everything bad that has happened to us"

"He only killed one family member and you murdered him first before that!" exclaimed Zachariah letting the anger he was brewing out in his speech

"Don't you raise your voice to me, you are a child and children will be compliant. Whenever I tell you something it's the truth and when you are told you can't do something its final you better complete the task. If I say you aren't doing something because I don't do it you best see that activity as a WE don't do that. I won't even get started on who you can and can't be around because that's determined on how I'm feeling about that person. I didn't get a say in raising you so I'm quite surprised that mouth never got you shot"

"My mother did quite fine without your help and I am not a child. I am your child but even that's debatable when you look at my upbringing. Now answer the question Aerius"

"What's the question Zachariah?" Aerius said as he bite his tongue patiently waiting for his chance to strike

"Why Blame John Harkness for everything when a lot of the actions and murders are your fault and doing?" said Zachariah finally wanting to know what truly happened the night he was brought over to help hoist the rope that held John.

"The Blacksmith convinced my wife she did not have to believe in God then followed it up by teaming up with natives to scalp Levi in front of the whole town. He followed that up by stealing my little girl from me and ruining her life by putting that abomination inside her, he even wore Ambrose down until he died of heart complications, John

Harkness killed my brother and Joseph in one night, Look at what he did to Simeon" pointing over to Simeon's dead body Aerius tried to get Zachariah to look but his head wouldn't even give a small swivel

"Father you are manipulative and controlling!" howled Zachariah trying to be as loud as he could along with enunciating every word clearly "John didn't do half those things you claim; in fact you did almost all of that yourself. You didn't kill Eliphaz or Joseph those two death were John but Ambrose and Estelle are on you be a man of God and own up to your mistakes"

"I didn't make a mistake he really did those things!" stomping his feet pouting Aerius felt a hand on his left shoulder which claimed him to the point he looked drunk. He felt the hand of Jesus touch him and his soul was lifted "You know what I should be asking Jesus forgiveness for murdering my family rather than blaming it on John"

"There you go father let Jesus back into your heart allow the Holy Ghost to guide you and we can make the right decision together"

"It was me who would force Abigail to go to church and make my marriage unhappy and unpleasant to be in. It was I who set up Levi getting scalped, it was I who killed Estelle all become she fell in love. It was I that sent Ambrose to kill her and take away her final breathe."

"Keep going father you are getting a lot off your chest" as Aerius talked Zachariah just listened analyzing everything that was being said

"It was I who bought black widow poison from the native Natok and gave it to Joseph telling him to place it into a drink and give it to John. I even told the town that John murdered Estelle so they would allow me to hang him; once they allowed that I had Waylon unload multiple bullets into John's spine, after everyone lost interest and left, making sure he could not come back"

"You failed on that Father and now we have to find a better way to accomplish the task you couldn't complete" Zachariah lifted his arm placing it on Aerius's right shoulder he started for the left but changed last minute sensing another presence was there. "I shall leave you to breathe in the Holy Ghost and I will find out what's going on with John's eyes". Staying completely still Aerius felt the hand of a divine presence on his left shoulder he didn't feel worthy of God's at this moment he felt lost and abandoned without anyone. He now had Zachariah in his life just like he always wanted however he was a man now and all the time they could have bonded with each other had passed by making them strangers who share blood.

"Jesus I believe you love me! Please forgive me for my sins! Help me to be a better person. Amen" said Aerius as he clenched onto what little faith was still flaming deep inside his heart "Cari Deus, in spe abundamus virtute spiritus sancti tui. Omni gaudio et pace reple nos sicut in te credimus, Spiritus Sancte, Deus, Fac vitam nostram ad producendum fructum tuum dilectionis, gaudium, pacem, patientiam, benignitatem, bonitatem, fidelitatem, mansuetudinem, et continentiam." Feeling the Holy Ghost next to him Aerius walked to his podium over looking seven rows of empty pews the only person sitting in one was John and he was still in a catatonic state, Aerius didn't see Zachariah who said he was going to try and figure out what was happening to John.

Having to fly higher each time the broom was swung The crow perched itself right above the liquor bottles just looking at the Saloon Maiden. "Get your ass away from my bottles!" screamed the Saloon Maiden as she reached for the shot gun under the bar not remembering it wasn't their anymore. "You lucky I ain't got my gun" the crow soared down tapping its feet on the bottle tops cawing as it flew back to its perch. "So you listened and didn't die, Take one" finally seeing that the crow's eyes were Johns' the saloon Maiden lifted a bottle for the crow to fly off with. Once it arrived at the church Aerius tried to capture it in his bare hands not knowing it was linked to John. Flying low enough to drop the bottle into John's lap the crow flew off and when it was completely out of sight John's eyes reappeared.

"Finally a drink" ripping the cork out of the bottle John gulped every drop as fast as he could.

"You shouldn't be drinking Harkness but it is fitting you had your final drink"

"Aerius you best claim that ass down before I beat you senseless"

"I have had my faith in Christ renewed by the Holy Ghost none of your false threats can harm me" Aerius was still standing behind his podium it looked as though he was preaching a surname to John

"So you just read another fairytale, I'm just glad you can read"

"Your jokes don't amuse me and I will not encourage the notation"

"So are you the hero now? You still look like the villain to me who kills their kin then can't take the blame" John stood up walking up the podium "Your faith is a mask and you know your soul won't ever be saved you are too far gone"

"God has forgiven me and he will forgive you too"

"I'd rather die for good" said John sarcastically as he reached for Aerius's shirt

"you cannot teach me I am a man of Christ"

"I don't care if you are a man who loves his vanity more than people I can still strangle you" reaching for Aerius's shirt to yank him close

John kept missing, he could be inches away and still miss just shaking the shirt with a breeze

"I told you" laughed Aerius

"So John's up good we can end him now" said Zachariah as he reentered the room "I hope your journey back to Jesus was a good one Father"

"It was blessed my son, I can feel him with me as clear as I can feel you here. I feel amazing"

"That is good Father now let's use this follow me" Zachariah placed a small box on the podium and set his sights on to John

"What's wrong problem you seemed just fine with me early. If you wanted to die I could have kill you on the walk from the Sawmill"

"I am honoring my father just like the bible says to do and he wants you dead so that is how I'll honor him" Grabbing John by the back of his arms pulling him down to his knees Zachariah waved Aerius over "bring the box and those matches" Zachariah held onto John as he thrashed around trying to break free, He didn't try to stand up he only thought about being able to use his arms and fist

"They are here in my hand, where do you want them Zachariah?"

"It's just one giant stick not a box of multiple"

"Where do you want it then?"

"In his mouth" said Zachariah as he begin to struggle he didn't know how much longer he could hold back John

"In his mouth, are you sure?"

"YES PUT THE DYNAMITE IN HIS MOUTH" Aerius punched John in his stomach so he would be winded and open his mouth "We can force it" cupping his hand around John's jaw forcing it down causing his mouth to open Aerius Shoved the large stick of dynamite right down his throat. The stick was shoved at an uncomfortable angle causing parts of It to stick out along with the wick. "You need to light the fuse father" Aerius sparked one of the matches he had using it to ignite the wick of the dynamite.

"We should run!" Yelled Aerius darting to hide behind his podium

"Yes I have to let go but I have a few seconds" pulling the rope John kept around his waist Zachariah tied his hands together "Good luck coming back from this" running from John to behind the podium with Aerius "I wanted to see the show"

"It's going to take awhile my son" just as Aerius looked away John's head exploded sending pieces all over the church "The demon is finally gone"

"Not yet father we must complete the crucifixion you tried to do"

"I know the perfect spot follow me with what's left" picking up John's body throwing it over his shoulder Zachariah followed Aerius down a dimly lit hallway leading to a door. "This is where I keep everything that's important" seeing inside Zachariah's stomach dropped he had just watched a man's head get blow off and now he smelled rotten flesh.

"Who's that on the floor?"

"That's Abigail she made it highly known she'd never believe in Christ again"

"So you killed her?"

"She had it coming. That was an old me come on let's not dwell on the past" grabbing nails off his work bench Aerius instructed Zachariah to place John's body on the floor "it'd be easier to nail with the body on the ground"

"If it's a crucifixion you'll need a cross to nail him to"

"I have just the thing" Aerius walked going into the room where he had Estelle's body looking for his wooden cross

"You need help in there?"

"No, I have it!" going to help Aerius anyway Zachariah pulled back the curtain and saw Estelle's decomposing corpse perched in a chair

"What the fuck did I just see?"

"Nothing, you don't belong in this room"

"Don't belong? You have Estelle's dead body" Zachariah dropped off John's body and stepped over Abigail's mutilated body. "What is going through your head?" finding his way over to the table to see Aerius it soon become known that Zachariah was going to have to fight his way out of the cellar room if he wanted to live. Aerius already has an appetitive for killing and he seems to prefer his family member.

"I'm about to put the nails into his wrist and feet help me out" holding a nail above John's wrist Aerius started to hammer slowly watching the nail disappear, he repeated this method until John's headless body was completely crucified.

"I hope you enjoy seeing that"

"Having him on my wall shows Harkness can never come back" walking over picking up Abigail's body Aerius chained it back up "I'm sorry I didn't put you back after our night together" waving for

Zachariah to come over "I want you to meet someone come here" rushing over to Aerius he did not aspect who he was about to be introduced to

"Who do I need to meet father?"

"Abigail this is my son Zachariah, His mother is Rebekah the women I had an affair with" looking at Abigail it was easy to pick out bruises from cut marks and where she had been abused before death "Say hello to her Zachariah"

"Hello Abigail I hope your night is going good" said Zachariah unsure what to say in a situation like this. He had seen dead bodies but this was the first time he was told to greet one that was chained underneath a church

"I can't ask Zachariah that, he's fragile he wouldn't know how to take it"

"Wouldn't know how to take what?"

"Abigail wanted to if you'd ever been with a dead body"

"Been with a dead body?"

"Yes she wanted to know if you've had intercourse with a dead body"

"HELL NO! That's not something I'm in to. I'm only still here because you are my father"

"Don't yell at me, Abigail I told you that he wouldn't be okay with it" Aerius was pressed up against Abigail believing he could still hear her.

"Aerius I think it's time you have to get rid of her body"

"She's still alive just sleeping, we are okay....We are okay" Aerius grabbed Abigail's hand feeling how cold her skin was "He wants me to get rid of you but he doesn't understand you aren't gone"

"That's a corpse"

"She's my everything son I don't have anyone else"

"You have me now so you don't have to keep her dead body. I'll help you bury her"

"Where would we bury her?"

"Right down here that way she is always close to you"

"I can do that" Grabbing shovels Aerius and Zachariah started digging a hole in the ground "She may have turned her back on Jesus but I never turned my body on her"

"You still love her?"

"I will always love her"

"The way John loved Estelle?"

"Those two had something special" Aerius stopped shoveling and thought about the turmoil he brought to both Estelle and John before they were both killed.

"I think this is deep enough. Help me with her body" Zachariah grabbed Abigail's corpse by the torso and Aerius grabbed to it by the waist and legs "Do you want to say anything or just throw dirt and cover her up?" Asked Zachariah

"I'd prefer to just fill the hole up with dirt" said Aerius as he took a fist full kissed his fist and threw it inside the hole covering Abigail's body.

"You are a brave man father"

"Why must you be a kiss ass Zachariah did your mother raise you that way?"

"She died when I was six if you really must know most of my upbringing and rising came from your sermons so yes I was raised that way… That way by you"

"Keep that attitude up and you'll end up in that hole with Abigail"

"So on that note I'm leaving"

"Just leave me like everyone else"

"You're not going to guilt trip me into staying father I'm leaving" opening the door for Zachariah to leave just like he wants Aerius pulled a blade and stabbed him in the side multiple times.

"What guilt trip? You can't leave me, everyone wants to leave me"

"You have your faith that should be enough" Zachariah closed his eyes and died right at Aerius's foot.

"Faith only gets me so far and I'm so sorry Abigail" Aerius walked over to the hole he and Zachariah dug for Abigail's body and wipe the dirt off her face placing a kiss on her lips. "Why doesn't anyone want to stay with me? Am I really that bad?" using his bare hands to dig up Abigail's corpse chaining it back up. "I am so sorry he got me to do that" Aerius sat on the floor with his head against Abigail's feet. "Please Jesus stop testing me with tribulations I just want to be happy in life"

Chapter 9: Over the Veil

As John opened his eyes he found himself surround by pitch black shadows and he could feel water under his feet with every step he took not knowing where he was he just walked forward. Having no clue which direction was which he stopped and shouted "Is anymore out there?"

"So you went ahead and died just like I told you not to, You really are smart" the words came from a voice allured by the shadows John couldn't see anything but he did recognize the voice it was the same voice from when he got cut down the second time. He was afraid that he may end up seeing her again but this was the afterlife and last he checked the woman was still alive.

"Where are you?" blurted John loudly trying to use the echoes of his voice to pick up sound waves to determine where the woman who belonged to the voice he was hearing was. His hearing had never faltered as a blacksmith with each swing of his hammer onto red hot steal he learned that each hit had a different sound and when he dip the scolding metal into water it bubbled and hissed each time differently. It was this skill he was using to try and pin point the figure in the darkness. Instead of his shop hammer he was attempting to use his voice hoping the echoes would disrupt the water he felt beneath his feet and create tiny rippling waves that would help him detect where the voice was coming from in the dark. As he peered into pitch black not a single human shaped silhouette could be made out no matter the direction he looked. John only saw pitch darkness, a darkness that would make a starry night blush, he tried shifting his eyes all around attempting to notice anything but all that was surrounding him was pitch black emptiness engulfed by an endless darkness.

"You dead now" the voice said as a soft tapping sound started. It sounded like a faint clock in the distance but John couldn't figure out why he'd be hearing a clock even if it's just the faint ticking of one. The ticking was so faint it almost couldn't be made out however the soft sound grew louder as John listened to it. His ears fixated on each tick hoping to make out which direction it was coming from. It wasn't until the ticking turned into even louder chiming that John could tell the sound was directly in front of his face.

"I can do better if I'm given another chance" pleaded John having no clue on how he was even able to die, he knew one day he'd expire and finally die but he didn't believe that too much damage from wounds would be able to send him to the afterlife. If this was the afterlife he was in all he could see was darkness. Each time the Crow took human form to help John she would warn him not to take too much damage and he would never heed her warning. This wasn't just her blowing smoke at him she was truly WARNING him since unbeknownst to John healing was never meant to be part of his supernatural gifts. Each wound that he received during his fights was meant to stay visible and not heal. They would act as a reminder his time on earth was barrowed time. The Crow however knew John would be careless since she could sense his heart of fueled by Revenge and Vengeance, This prompted her to give his body the power to regenerate from non-fatal wounds.

"You want another chance to do what die again? Did you even get vengeance?" the voice sounded closer and the tapping had gotten louder. The woman could reach in the darkness and touch John although she just stood next to him allowing him to vocally grovel and plea for another chance. She got enjoyment out of watching him be like this since he never wanted to heed her warnings. The loud ticking was from a pocket watch the woman was dangling in front of John's face. She had altered the pocket watch to chime like a grandfather clock each time an hour passed, she believed the louder the chime in pitch black the more frightened John would start to become and maybe he'd realize his own mistakes.

"I was killed by the man who killed my love what do you think?" exclaimed John as he placed his hands over his face trying to hide the fact he was crying. Inside he was destroyed and on the outside he was finally showing it.

"I think your black ass kept getting hurt and I had to bail you out" the woman said her tone was so sarcastic John felt like a dagger was stabbed in his heart. The ticking stopped and no loud chime could be heard the darkness was once again silent.

"Bail me out?" John asked confused as he walked through his hands still using them to hide the fact he was crying.

"Yeah bail your ass out" as the room started to fill with light John seen the woman, it was the same woman who cut him down when Ambrose hung him, he was able to figure out it was her from her voice but the look on her face was new to him. She had disappointment and pity on her face when she looked at him "This is your last chance Jonathan you'll only be able to die once As though you were a mortal man so make it count" the woman didn't want to give John anymore chances but the crow spirit that used her body as a vessel wanted to see how sending him back would pan out. The Crow had never resurrected anyone before and was using John as its guinea pig to work out the kinks.

"You won't regret this" nervously said John as his body filled with excitement. He was going to go after Pastor Aerius once he got to the land of the living and that would complete his need for vengeance.

"I best not or I'll kill your ass" the woman sternly warned John and he knew it wasn't an empty threat although he felt deep down as long as he got vengeance for Estelle the woman would be okay with whatever happens to him. He could still feel the love she carried for her late husband and knew the only reason she kept helping was because she loved to see young people that were in love get their happy ending.

"When can I go back?" said John full of eager excitement that he was given a final chance. He wanted to return as fast as possible in order to get vengeance and he couldn't wait any longer to be able to kill Pastor Aerius

"Someone wants to see you first before you go" remarked the woman reaching her hand into the only spot of darkness left guiding someone from it.

"Who wants to see me?" everything went silent as a figure wearing a shroud walked up to john when she took her hood off John fell to his knees before regaining his balance. He couldn't believe who he was looking at it had to be impossible but here she was.

"Hello Johnny I've missed you" said Estelle as she leaned in to kiss him. John leaned into the kiss missing how soft Estelle's lips were.

"I missed you so much Estelle I can't believe I get to see you" John wrapped his arms around Estelle embracing her passionately "I'm so glad I get to see you before I go back" burying his head in her neck John found himself not wanting to go back he only wanted to be with Estelle. She had been as beautiful as the first day he saw her and now he had her once again but at what cost this time. John had already begged to return to earth and finish his plot for vengeance however after seeing Estelle he didn't want to leave from her arms.

"Go take care of your unfinished business and I'll be here waiting my love" said Estelle as she slide her hand up John's back resting her hand on his head "I'll be waiting for you so hurry up" holding the only man she ever loved while being in the afterlife felt dreadful, it wasn't her fault that they were here but she felt at fault since if she never loved John they both would be alive. Loving John was the best thing Estelle ever did and she wouldn't change any part of it accept for their deaths.

"I'll be as fast as I can my love, we will be together again" said John before he started to kiss Estelle not knowing the next time he'd get to do so

"This is all great but that clock is ticking Romero so let's get a move on" the woman walked over to John and with the wave of her hand she opened a Veil for him to go back through. As the veil opened John became overcome by the feeling of abandonment not being sure if he'd ever return to be with Estelle. He didn't want her to see that he had doubts on whether or not he would be able to return to her.

"I had my head blown off, how does that work?" asked John his arms still wrapped around Estelle, having her in his arms was a feeling he never wanted to forget, He could feel her heart beat in sync with his and that feeling made everything seem alright even when nothing was.

"You had what blown off?" the woman raised one eyebrow looking at John in complete shock. She couldn't believe what he just said

"My head was blown off" repeated John shrugging his shoulders "I don't know how that'll work" Estelle pulled from John only holding his hand briefly as she stepped away from him. She knew it was his time to return and thus got out the way for an easier transition

"How'd your dumb ass get your head blown off?" the woman asked shock still on her face. She still couldn't wrap her mind around the fact John went a got his head blown off.

"Aerius stuck a dynamite stick in my mouth while Zachariah held my arms then boom I'm here" John didn't seem fazed anymore about the type of wounds people inflicted on him; he had become numb to it all.

"I'll have to increase the amount of power you have for that head to grow back" the woman didn't want to send John back without a head although she also didn't want to send him back having access to more power than he needed.

"You can do that?" asked John who was now the confused one

"I'm going to have to" the woman grabbed John and drew the power from her body transmitting it into his by doing this she insured that John's head would regenerate when he walked through the veil. She knew that doing a power transfer would take everything she had left in her leaving only that little timid woman that everyone walked all over "Don't waste it"

"I won't waste the power you gave me, I'm ready" said John

"You will regain the power of the crow for 24 hours then regardless you will die so make it count" As John walked up to the veil he thought about so much he wanted to say to Estelle that the woman had to reopen the veil several time each time draining more and more of her life force

"You need to go finish so we can be together" said Estelle as she placed a gently kiss onto John cheek

"Estelle you are correct when the veil opens I'll go" seeing the veil open John put one hand in "One last kiss? That cheek wasn't enough"

Estelle ran over to give John a final kissed "I can't leave you behind" pulling Estelle through the veil with him was John's final straw.

Chapter 10: Goodbye Pastor

Opening his eyes wide to a downward view John had no idea where he was "What have you done to my body Aerius?" yelled John as he turned his head left to right seeing he was nailed up on the wall "So am I just some game hunt to you?"

"You are meant to be dead" pulling a gun on John cocking it back ready to shot Aerius was stopped after hearing one word. At first he thought his mind was playing tricks on him but he had to go find out.

"Daddy" Cried Estelle her soul had gone back to her body which had spent time rotting away. "I'm scared Daddy it's so dark here" being able to smell the rotten flesh of her body Estelle begin to freak out. The only thing she remembered was John pulling her through the veil with him. She couldn't feel any of her body and if she went to move skin would drop off or bones would break having become so fragile just being staged in a chair. "Daddy I'm afraid Help me" cried Estelle she didn't want answers she just wanted to return to the afterlife where her soul now belonged

"You'll be okay princess Daddy is here. The lord as brought you back to me" preached Aerius as he ran into the other room seeing his baby girl alive once again. "You haven't changed one bit princess" walking over to Estelle with tears in his eyes Aerius didn't know what to say so he took her hand into his. When he lifted Estelle's hand the skin from her palm stuck to the chair that her body was staged in "Just open your heart to God and he will heal that" keeping Estelle's hand in his Aerius was just happy that he had his daughter back "Princess Did God restore your soul to your body?"

"John pulled me with him, why can't I feel anything? Daddy I'm scared" as Estelle started to panic her loud screams and cries kept Aerius by her side he didn't think about John he just wanted to make sure his daughter was okay after just returning from the dead. "Why can't I feel anything Daddy what happened to me?" Estelle cried to Aerius making sure he stayed by her side. She wasn't able to see John but knew if he was near he'd need a distraction so that he could escapes from whatever contraption he was put in. "DADDY DON'T LEAVE ME!" emotionally screamed Estelle when Aerius was about to leave the room, lifting her arm watching the flesh just melt off she reached out grabbing Aerius shirt seeing his daughter's arm and how much of her skin was gone Aerius pulled away not wanting to be touched by her "Daddy don't you love me won't you help me" Estelle reached more and more for Aerius until he was backed against the wall without any way to move or exit. This gave John enough time to rip his wrist past the nails that had been put in them. Landing on the ground trying to be as quite as he could John walked to the room Estelle was in.

"Hello Aerius!" John said with a smooth tone "I believe it's your turn" grabbing Aerius by his neck dragging him over "Time to build a shine to me using you as my center piece"

"I need to help Estelle my fight with you is 2nd when it comes to her" Aerius tried to break free of John's hold so that he could help his daughter even with the fact her rotten flesh revolted him. The hold that John had him in was to strong and he couldn't budge.

"She'll be okay we will return once my vengeance is completed" throwing Aerius onto the cross John could feel he finally had the right guy vengeance was finally his and it felt bittersweet. He was killing the man who murdered his love and framed him for it and he was crucifying a man who put Christ before everyone even his own family it was poetic justice.

"Johnny what's going on? I'm afraid" cried Estelle from the room where her rotten corpse sat she could feel more of herself rotten away as the time by

"Just finally getting my vengeance on your killer my love" placing the first nail onto Aerius's wrist John used his strength to drive it through until it went completely into the wood repeating this until Aerius was crucified looking like the lord he served

"You won't get away with this John Harkness" said Aerius as he watched his blood drip down onto his bible unbeknownst to John

"I just did Pastor Aerius Ridgeway; You've preached your last sermon" leaving Aerius bleeding out John walked in the room where Estelle's body was rotting away "We can go home now" being gentle as he scooped Estelle into his arms John walked towards a dirt wall knowing there was an open veil. Carrying Estelle in his arm John whisked her off to the afterlife where they could finally be together without anyone trying to radical them.

Chapter 11: Reaper's Vow

Seeing the veil shut behind them Estelle and John didn't feel happy they could tell something was wrong but didn't know what it was. "You got your vengeance but at what cost John?" The woman's voice could be heard once again but it was faint and her voice once powerful was now quite

"Why is it always you?" remarked John who was still holding Estelle bridal style. He didn't care much for the woman anymore after she only seemed to show up after he was in trouble and not before to leaned a hand. John didn't want to answer anything she wanted to know he just wanted to spend his days in the afterlife with his beloved.

"You need me so answer me!" remarked the woman her face still showing disappoint but she was grinding her teeth as she spoke due to how infuriated she was at John.

"There was no cost just vengeance" the woman who had been helping John did not like his response and she let her fury free. First she restored Estelle's body so that John didn't have to carry her then she unloaded an armadas worth of punches onto John letting out all her pent up anger over his actions.

"Your happiness was at risk and you destroyed it!" continuing to punch John the woman noticed her punches were becoming more powerful, stopping so she could figure out why she noticed that John's face had blood all over it from a bloody nose. When his blood got on her the power that she gave John was being transferred back to her.

"John destroyed our happiness how?" Watching the woman punch John over and over until he was a bloody mess Estelle wanted to know how her happiness with John was destroyed.

"He took you back with him once he took your soul off this plain it cost your happiness" the woman answered Estelle's questions as he punched John one last time.

"It can't be that bad we can just rekindle things here in the afterlife" said John grabbing Estelle's hand pulling her close. "We have our whole afterlife to be together our happiness will be fine" said John as he looked Estelle in her eyes feeling more in love with her in that moment than he ever had before.

"You aren't the smartest John" The woman remarked sarcastically as John started shaking his head he was getting angry he wanted to know what was going on and not have riddles.

"Just tell me" remarked John letting his tone slip out

"Estelle stays here, you have to go back" said the woman through her teeth feeling like John had just been using her for the fact she was watching over him. She had saved him multiple times and even taken out her aggression on him but nothing could prepare her for how Estelle was going to act to the news.

"John has more vengeance to take out on guys?" Estelle asked having no idea what John had already been put through. "Can we skip the vengeance and he just stay with me?" Estelle asked grabbing John by his arm

"He will be guiding those who come back so that they don't make his mistakes!" said the woman as she looked directly at John and Estelle "Hopefully they won't need you to rescue them as much as you needed me to rescue you!"

"So eternal youth I can handle that while helping people" shaking his head with confidence thinking it'd be a breeze John's mood changed once he heard what would really happen

"You don't have eternal youth you'll still age and then your skin will fall off until your just bone" the woman found herself smirking at the thought of John slowly becoming just a skeleton unrecognizable to anyone.

"I'm being made into a grim reaper for birds?" John went to go hit the woman out of anger but she didn't flinch what caused him to stop just before he connected

"You have a set of balls Cowboy but settle that ass down before I remind you what pain is really like when I'm the one throwing the punches" looking into Estelle's eyes John no longer saw any love what emotions he had towards her were all destroyed when he took her soul through the veil without her being allowed.

"Take me back to earth without love here what's the point" holding his head down mopping towards the veil he was stopped the woman had instructions for him that must be followed

"Remember they can't bring loved ones back from the dead and they must take vengeance on the true killer" hearing the woman loud and clear John was just readying to go, he was destined to become a skeleton and guide others to what he no longer had. Those were years he just wanted to get through.

"I understand…" As john walked through the veil Estelle lost all memories of him and went off to heaven. John stepped out right where he left seeing Aerius dead from bleeding out. "I liked what she called me before I left…Cowboy that'll help hide my true name from the world" walking around Aerius's church cellar room John found a black trench coat and an all black cowboy hat hidden away behind an old piano that was stacked with boxes of bibles "That'll fit but it's missing something". Looking up at Aerius and seeing the man who cost him everything John figured out the last thing he needed. "Until my flesh inevitably rots off I'll wear yours" picking up the cross holding Aerius to bring it down closer to him John placed his hand over Aerius face ripping it off "Not the face a better piece is right here" breaking off the front of Aerius's Skull placing it over his face using a thin strain of thread.

Taking one final look in the mirror wearing Aerius's skull over his face, the black cowboy hat and the jet black trench coat it was at that time he knew Jonathan Harkness was no more and only "The Skull Cowboy" lived.

Snippet of Skull Cowboy: Scripture of Blood

Chapter 1: You've preached your last sermon

As John walked away he could feel Pastor Aerius's warm blood on his face. His journey on the mortal plan had just begun. He was now the messenger for the crow and his job was to worn anyone else who was resurrected about the dangers of doing what you want. They weren't allowed to stray from their path or attempt to bring the love of their life back to life. They were to strictly stay on their path for revenge or vengeance any deviations would result in dire consequences.

   What John didn't see was the albino crow that flew into the church cellar just as the doorway was buried by dirt being sealed off from the world. The Albino Crow perched itself on the old piano and looked at Pastor Aerius's dead body. The final thing the pastor saw was burnt into his eyes and the Albino Crow was fixated on it. The final image he saw caused a burning rage to build in his soul tethering it to the mortal plan even with his body destroyed. He had the face of John Harkness burnt into his retinas. The Albino Crow flew over landing on Pastor Aerius's body picking at the open flesh where his face once was. The more the Albino Crow picked at what was left the more flesh grew back this went on until the front of Pastor Aerius's skull reformed and his face regenerated. Hearing the cawing of the Albino Crow that was perched on his chest Pastor Aerius opened his eyes wide looking down to see the bird. "How is this possible?" he said out loud just before he started to feel the pain in his wrist. Being the only one in the Church's cellar he got no response only a single caw from the Albino Crow who had flown down to his left wrist and was peeking at the nails. "Hoc possum vincere dolorem" screamed Pastor Aerius as he forcefully prided his left wrist off of the cross John had nailed him to. He could feel every bit of pain as the nail was extracted from the wood staying inside his wrist. "I'll keep this as a memento" he remarked looking at the nail protruding from his wrist. The Albino Crow had moved over the Pastor Aerius's right wrist peeking out the nail he had in that wrist. Pulling his right wrist from the wood faster he noticed the pain had gone away but the nails were still in his wrist. "Dominus reduxit me ex causa, Quae causa sit, adhuc invenio, utcumque hanc secundam vitam accipiam, et doctrinas tuas mundo praedicabo" exclaimed Pastor Aerius out loud as though he was talking to God. "I am your servant Lord" he cried pulling the nails from his wrist "Your only son died for my sins before I was even born. Jesus gave his life for everyone, you gave your only son so that everyone would see his teaching were true. What did I do that granted me to come back to life?" Pastor Aerius watched as the wounds on his wrist healed he had only seen healing that fast on John. The Albino Crow flew backwards landing back on the piano cawing at Pastor Aerius fluttering its wings. "Quare resurrexisti me et fecisti me sicut creaturam illam abominabilem Johannem Harkness Dominum?" screamed Pastor Aerius, He never wanted to question the actions of his lord but what was happening to him wasn't something he understood so he had to question it. As the room fell silent the Albino Caw started cawing rapidly and flying towards Pastor Aerius's face causing him to duck and turn around. When he rose back up he was gazing at his reflection in a dust covered mirror, he couldn't believe what he was seeing not only did he come back to life but he was also younger. Leaning closer into the mirror Pastor Aerius caught the fading image of John Harkness that had been burnt into his retinas and he realized why he came back from the dead. "John was resurrected with an appetite for vengeance on me for murdering Estelle…. I've been resurrected to take revenge on John Harkness for what he did to my family"

Pastor Aerius used his sleeve to wipe some of the dust off the mirror to get a better look at his reflection. "A villain in someone else's story but a hero in his own" the words echoed behind Pastor Aerius he continued to check out his reflection.

"John claimed I was the villain in his story and even killed me for it but NOW I'VE RETURNED! He can't play the HERO ANYMORE since I control the ink that writes my story" proudly said Pastor Aerius as he turned from the mirror and walked over to the boxes on top of the piano. "These will come in handy to preach to the world. Preaching before brought John to me and I'll use it again" as he pulled the box of bibles off of the piano the bottom gave out sending the books crashing to the floor.

"Preach all you want Aerius"

"Who's talking? I thought I was alone here" said Pastor Aerius as he finally heard the voice, he didn't notice it the first time but he could hear the thick English accent now and it startled him. "In the name of Jesus Christ reveal thy self"

"I'm your guide your totem to the afterlife" spoke the voice "I am the reason you return to the living, I saw the thrist for revenge that stained your soul"

"How do you see something like that?" Pastor Aerius asked lifting his stack of bibles.

"Your eyes said it al when I got here but your spirit was screaming for a way to return so you could get revenge on John Harkness" the voice was right behind Pastor Aerius and he could feel breathe on the back of his name. "I figured taking human form would be better for you" placing his hand on Pastor Aerius's shoulder spinning him around the voice shifted back into the Albino Crow just as he was meet by Pastor Aerius's eyes.

"You're the bird that's been cawing?" laughed Pastor Aerius as he begun to grab his wrist the wounds had reopened and he could feel the pain.

"Remember I control weather you heal or not so keep the comments to yourself" the voice was now a man standing right in front of Pastor Aerius. "You can go preach your gospel all you want. Revenge doesn't have an expiration date but just know this more than one day has gone by" the man shifted back into the Albino Crow and threw out of the church cellar through a tiny that had broken through the dirt.

"What do you mean by more than one day?" questioned Pastor Aerius he didn't understand what that meant although before he had any chance dirt fell on top of him and he could see light shinning in.

"STOP THE DIGGER I SEE SOMEONE!" screamed a construction worker signaling for the machine to be turned off. "Hey buddy who are you and how'd you get down there?"

"I am Pastor Aerius and the Lord put me here"

"The lord put you there? And what lord would this be?" the foreman had come over when the digger was stopped and he was the one to spoke to Pastor Aerius. "You and your lord have to go this is a dig site and we got work to do"

"This is my home I own this church" exclaimed Pastor Aerius pointing to where his church once was.

"Buddy their hasn't been a church here in seventy years"

"No church what does everyone do one Sundays without one?" climbing through the hole made by the digger Pastor Aerius started handing out the bibles he had. "We don't need a church I can preach without one"

"We watch football and no one here wants your dusty books!" angrily spoke the foreman

"These aren't busty books it's the word of Christ"

"Word of Christ looks like a dusty ass book to me" hearing this man talk about the bible the way he did angered Pastor Aerius. Lifting a bible to his lips kissing the tip Pastor Aerius gripped it tightly in his hands.

"I'm sorry for what's about to happen"

"You're going to be sorry if you don't leave my work site" remarked the foreman as he got angrier.

"Once again I'm Sorry" said Pastor Aerius as he kissed the bible

"You must really want an ass wiping after saying Sorry to me two" Pastor Aerius started laughed

"I was talking to the bible" jamming the bible at the foreman's throat Pastor Aerius didn't stop until the man's head went rolling in front of the digger. "I'd be upset to but nothing to lose your head over" waving the bloody bible at everyone on site around him "You will leave this place around or you'll feel the good book". Everyone scattered away from Pastor Aerius has he stood with a bloody bible in his hand. "I don't think Pastor Aerius Ridgeway fits in this new world" bringing the bible to his chin feeling the warm blood it was at that moment he knew Pastor Aerius Ridgeway was no more and only "Father Elric" lived.

Printed in Great Britain
by Amazon